LEARNING THROUGH PROJECT EULER

PART 1. THE FIRST 25 PROBLEMS OF PROJECT EULER

with programs in Pascal, C++ and Java

NGUYEN XUAN HUY

1957 <u>Soviet Union</u> stamp commemorating the 250th birthday of Euler.

The text says: *250 years from the birth of the great mathematician, academician Leonhard Euler.* (*From Internet, 2018*)

PREFACE

"*Project Euler* (named after Leonhard Euler) is a website dedicated to a series of computational problems intended to be solved with computer programs. The project attracts adults and students interested in computer science. Since its creation in 2001 by Colin Hughes, Project Euler has gained notability and popularity worldwide. It includes over 600 problems, with a new one added once every two weeks (except during the summer break). Problems are of varying difficulty, but each is solvable in less than a minute of CPU time using an efficient algorithm on a computer. Problems can be sorted on difficulty. A forum specific to each question may be viewed after the user has correctly answered the given question. As of August 2017, Project Euler has about 750,000 users, from all over the world, who have solved at least one problem.

Participants can track their progress through achievement levels based on the number of problems solved. A new level is reached for every 25 problems solved. Special awards exist for solving special combinations of problems, for instance there is an award for solving fifty prime numbered problems. A special Eulerians level exists to track achievement based on the fastest fifty solvers of recent problems so that newer members can compete without solving older problems.

There are over 100 sequences in the On-Line Encyclopedia of Integer Sequences (OEIS) referencing Project Euler problems."

From Wikipedia, the free encyclopedia, 2018

This little book gives solutions for the first twenty-five problems of the Project Euler.

The solutions are presented in the following form,

Problem

Understanding

Algorithm

Program in DevC++

Program in Free Pascal

Program in Blue J (Java)

The readers can load and install the programming environments of these languages at the following Internet addresses,

DevC++: http://www.bloodshed.net/index.html

Free Pascal: https://www.freepascal.org/

BlueJ: https://www.bluej.org/

Acknowledgments

First and foremost, I wish to express my gratitude to Nguyen Dang Binh and his helpful staff. They helped with everything to translate the original Vietnamese version to English. I greatly appreciate my colleague Vu Duy Man for his support and encouragement for this book. It gives me great joy to acknowledge the contributions of my brother, Nguyen Xuan Vinh, my nephew Phong Vinh Alphonse, and my nieces, Thuy Duong, and Hanh Quyen to the correction of English version. Most important, I thank my wife, Trung Thu, and our children, Thu Hang, and Xuan Hoang, for the world of love and happiness they share with me.

I have appreciated all the suggestions, corrections, and comments from users of previous Vietnamese editions of this book. Many of their ideas have been incorporated in this edition.

Finally, I thank in advance all those, who send me suggestions and corrections of this book in the future.

The Literature Temple Van Mieu, Hanoi, May 5, 2018

Nguyen Xuan Huy

E-mail: nxhuy564@gmail.com

HP : 84-903203800

CONTENTS

Problem 1. Sum

If we list all the natural numbers below 10 that are multiples of 3 or 5, we get 3, 5, 6 and 9. The sum of these multiples is 23.

Find the sum of all the multiples of 3 or 5 below 1000.

Understanding

Some definitions, including the standard ISO 80000-2 begin the natural numbers with 0, corresponding to the non-negative integers 0, 1, 2, 3, ..., whereas others start with 1, corresponding to the positive integers 1, 2, 3, ... In this book, we accept that the set of natural numbers is {1, 2, 3, ...}

Given integers $a > 0$ and b, we use the notation $a \mid b$ to indicate that a divides b, that is, b is a *multiple* of a. If $a \mid b$ then we know that there is some integer k, such that $b = ka$. If b is a *multiple* of a, then we also say that a is a *divisor* or *factor* of b. The problem says, "*Find the sum of all the multiples of 3 or 5 below* 1000." Note to the connective word "*or*" in the sentence.

Since 6 is a multiple of 3, 6 is added to the sum.

Since 10 is a multiple of 5, 10 is added to the sum.

Since 15 is a multiple of 3, 15 is added to the sum.

Since 15 is a multiple of 5, 15 is added to the sum.

Thus, 15 is *added twice* to the sum, hence we need to eliminate this case.

Algorithm

The result of the problem is $sum = T_3 + T_5 - T_{15}$, where,

T_3 is the sum of all the multiples of 3 below 1000:

$$T_3 = 3 + 6 + \ldots + 3a = 3(1 + 2 + \ldots + a); \ a = 999 \ \text{div} \ 3 = 333.$$

T_5 is the sum of all the multiples of 5 below 1000:

$$T_5 = 5 + 10 + \ldots + 5b = 5(1 + 2 + \ldots + b); \ b = 999 \ \text{div} \ 5 = 199.$$

T_{15} is the sum of all the multiples of $15 = 3 \times 5$ below 1000:

$T_{15} = 15 + 30 + \ldots + 15c = 15(1 + 2 + \ldots + c); c = 999$ div $15 = 66.$

When German mathematician Gauss was eight, he figured out how to get the sum of all the natural numbers from 1 to 100.

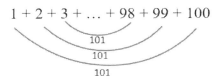

$$1 + 2 + 3 + \ldots + 98 + 99 + 100 = 101 \times 50 = 5050$$

In general, the sum of all the first n natural numbers is computed by the Gaussian formula, $G(n)$, as

$$G(n) = 1 + 2 + \cdots + n = \frac{n(n + 1)}{2} \qquad (Gauss)$$

So,

$$sum = T_3 + T_5 - T_{15} =$$
$$= 3*G(999 \text{ div } 3) + 5*G(999 \text{ div } 5) - 15*G(999 \text{ div } 15).$$

C++ Program

```
/*****************************************
  Problem 1. Sum
  Answer = 233168, Time = 0.12 sec.
*****************************************/
#include <iostream>
#include <windows.h>

using namespace std;

inline int G(int n) { return n*(n+1)/2; }

main() {
  int n = 1000-1;
  int E1 = 3*G(n/3) + 5*G(n/5) - 15*G(n/15);
  cout << E1; // 233168
  cout << "\n T H E    E N D . ";
  return 0;
}
```

Notes

- The `inline` functions are a C++ enhancement feature to increase the execution time of a program. When the inline function is called, whole code of the function gets inserted or substituted at the point of function call. This substitution is performed by the C++ compiler at compile time. Inline function may increase efficiency if it is small.

- In C++ if both numbers `x` and `y` are integers, then `x/y` is an integer.

Free Pascal Program

```
(* * * * * * * * * * * * * * * * * * * * * * * * * * * * * * * * * * * * *
  Problem 1.  Sum
  Answer = 233168, Time = 0.12 sec.
* * * * * * * * * * * * * * * * * * * * * * * * * * * * * * * * * * * * *)
type int = longint;
var n: int;

function G(n: int): int;
begin G := (n*(n+1) div 2); end;

BEGIN
  n := 1000-1;
  writeln(3*G(n div 3)+5*G(n div 5)
           -15*G(n div 15)); // 233168
  writeln(' T H E    N D .');
  readln;
END.
```

Note

In Pascal, the declaration

```
    type int = longint;
```

means the user-defined type `int` and the base type `longint` are the same. These types have size of 4 bytes and the value range -2147483648 to 2147483647.

Java Program

```
/*************************************
  Problem 1. Sum
  Answer = 233168, Time = 0.12 sec.
 *************************************/
public class E1 {
  private int n = 1000;

  E1() {
    n = n-1;
    System.out.println(3*G(n/3)+ 5*G(n/5)-
                       15*G(n/15));// 233168
  } // E1

  private int G(int n){ return (n*(n+1))/2; }
} // class E1
```

Problem 2. Even Fibonacci numbers

Each new term in the Fibonacci sequence is generated by adding the previous two terms. By starting with 1 and 2, the first 10 terms will be:

1, 2, 3, 5, 8, 13, 21, 34, 55, 89, ...

By considering the terms in the Fibonacci sequence whose values do not exceed four million, find the sum of the even-valued terms.

Understanding

Let $F = (c_1, c_2, ..., c_{10}, ...)$ be the Fibonacci sequence of the problem. We have

c_1	c_2	c_3	c_4	c_5	c_6	c_7	c_8	c_9	c_{10}
1	**2**	3	5	**8**	13	21	**34**	55	89

c_2, c_4, c_6, c_8 and c_{10} are the terms with *even indexes*, while $c_2 = $ **2**, $c_5 = $ **8**, and $c_8 = $ **34** are *even-valued terms* (they are underlined). Hence the sum of the even-valued terms below 100 is **2** + **8** + **34** = 44.

Algorithm

Consider the Fibonacci sequence starting with two numbers 1: 1, 1, **2**, 3, 5, **8**, 13, 21, **34**, 55, 89, **144**, ... where the even-valued terms are underlined. Note that after two odd-valued terms, we get an even-valued term. Now, we define by $o1$ and $o2$ the two adjacent odd-valued terms and by e the even-valued term after $o2$. Then the given Fibonacci sequence can be written by the following rhythm,

$$o1, o2, e, o1, o2, e, ...$$

Input: MN = 4000000.

$$c_1 = c_2 = 1; c_i = c_{i-2} + c_{i-1}, i > 2, c_i < MN$$

Output: sum $\{c_i \mid c_i < MN, c_i = 2k\}$.

```
begin
  // Initialize
  o1 ← 1; // the first odd-valued term
  o2 ← 1; // the second odd-valued term
  e ← o1 + o2; // e is the first even-valued term
  sum ← 0;
  while e < MN do
    sum ← sum + e;
    // compute the next (o1, o2, e)
    // from current (o1, o2, e)
    o1 ← o2 + e;
    o2 ← e + o1;
    e ← o1 + o2;
  endwhile
  return sum;
endE2
```

C++ Program

```cpp
/************************************************
   Problem 2. Even Fibonacci members < 4000000
   Answer = 4613732, Time = 0.1 sec.
 ************************************************/
#include <iostream>
#include <windows.h>

using namespace std;

const int MAXVAL = 4000000;

int E2() {
  int o1, o2; // adjacent odd-valued terms
  int e; // even-valued term e = o1 + o2
  int sum = 0;
  // Init
  o1 = o2 = 1;
  e = o1 + o2;
```

```
  while(e < MAXVAL) {
    sum += e;
    o1 = o2 + e;
    o2 = e + o1;
    e = o1 + o2;
  } // while
  return sum;
} // E2

main() {
  cout << E2(); // 4613732
  cout << "\n T H E    E N D.";
  return 0;
}
```

Free Pascal Program

```
(************************************************
  Problem 2. Even Fibonacci members < 4000000
  Answer = 4613732, Time = 0.1 sec.
*************************************************)
type int = longint;
const MAXVAL = 4000000;

function E2: int;
var
  o1, o2: int; // adjacent odd-valued terms
  e: int; // the even-valued terme = o1+o2
  sum: int;
begin
  // Init
  o1 := 1; o2 := 1; e := o1 + o2;
  sum := 0;
  while(e < MAXVAL) do
  begin
    sum := sum + e;
    o1 := o2 + e;
    o2 := o1 + e;
    e  := o1 + o2;
  end; // while
  exit(sum);
end; // E2

BEGIN
```

```
  writeln(E2); // 4613732
  writeln(' T H E    E N D. ');
  readln;
END.
```

Java Program

```
/************************************************
  Problem 2. Even Fibonacci numbers < 4000000
  Answer = 4613732, Time = 0.1 sec.
************************************************/
public class E2 {
  E2(){
    int o1,o2; // adjacent odd-valued term
    int e; // even-valued term e = o1 + o2
    int maxval = 4000000;
    int sum = 0;
    o1 = o2 = 1;
    e = o1 + o2;
    while (e < maxval) {
      sum += e;
      o1 = e + o2;
      o2 = e + o1;
      e = o1 + o2;
    } // while
    System.out.println(sum); // 4613732
  } // E2
} // class E2
```

Problem 3. Largest prime factor

The prime factors of 13195 are 5, 7, 13 and 29.

What is the largest prime factor of the number 600851475143?

Understanding

A *prime* is an integer greater than 1 that is divisible by no positive integers other than 1 and itself.

An integer greater than 1 that is not prime, is called *composite*. Thus, the set of all positive integers is a union of three disjoint subsets, namely,

- the set {1}. Note that 1 has only *one divisor* which is itself.
- the set of all primes {2, 3, 5, ...}. Note that every prime has *exactly two (different) divisors,* which are 1 and itself.
- the set of all composite numbers {4, 6, 8, 9, ...}. Note that every composite number has *more than two divisors*.

It is well-known the following results from elementary number theory,

☞ *i.* Every positive integer greater than one has a prime divisor.

☞ *ii.* There are infinitely many primes.

☞ *iii.* A positive integer n is a composite if and only if n has a prime factor not exceeding $\sqrt{n}$.

☞ *iv.* 2 is a unique even prime.

☞ *v.* 2 is the smallest prime.

☞ *vi.* All primes greater than 2 are odd numbers.

The Fundamental Theorem of Arithmetic (The Prime Factorization)

Every positive integer greater than one can be written uniquely as a product of primes in order of nondecreasing values.

$$n = p_1^{m_1} p_2^{m_2} \cdots p_k^{m_k} \tag{3.1}$$

where $k > 0$, $p_1 < p_2 < \ldots < p_k$ are primes, $m_i \geq 1$ and it is called the *degree* of prime factor p_i in n, $1 \leq i \leq k$.

Examples

126 = $2 \times 3^2 \times 7$, degree(2, 126) = 1, degree(3, 126) = 2, degree(7, 126) = 1.

153 = $3^2 \times 17$, degree(3, 153) = 2, degree(17, 153) = 1.

Algorithm

Let (3.1) be the prime factorization of n. Denote by,

$$n_1 = n = p_1^{m_1} p_2^{m_2} \cdots p_k^{m_k}$$

$$n_2 = n_1 \ div \ p_1^{m_1} = p_2^{m_2} \cdots p_k^{m_k}$$

. . .

$$n_k = n_{k-1} \ div \ p_{k-1}^{m_{k-1}} = p_k^{m_k}$$

In general,

$$n_i = n_{i-1} \ div \ p_{i-1}^{m_{i-1}} = p_i^{m_i} \cdots p_k^{m_k}, 2 \le i \le k.$$

Starting from $n_1 = n$, we consider each number p, $2 \le p \le int(\sqrt{n})$, where $int(x)$ is the integer part of a real number x. If $p \mid n_i$ then we set $p_i = p$ and compute $n_{i+1} = n_i \ div \ p_i^{m_i}$, where m_i is the degree of p_i in n_i. At the end of the process, we distinguish two cases:

Case 1. $n_i = 1$: we get p_{i-1} as the largest prime factor of n.

Case 2. $n_i > 1$: then n_i is the largest factor of n.

The next examples illustrate how to use prime factorization for the problem.

Example 1

$n = 126$. We have $int(\sqrt{n}) = 11$ and will scan p from 2 to 11.

$n_1 = 126$.

- $p = 2$. Since $2 \mid 126$, we get $p_1 = 2$, $m_1 = 1$, $n_2 = n_1 \ div \ 2$ = 126 div 2 = 63.

- $p = 3$. Since $3 \mid 63$, we get $p_2 = 3$, $m_2 = 2$, $n_3 = n_2 \ div \ 3^2$ = 63 div 9 = 7.

- All numbers p from 4 to 6 do not divide 7.

- $p = 7$. Since $7 \mid 7$, we get $p_3 = 7$, $m_3 = 1$, $n_4 = n_3$ div $7 =$
  $= 7$ div $7 = 1$.

The scanning process is broken at $n_4 = 1$ and we get the largest prime factor $p_3 = 7$.

Moreover, we also get the prime factorization of 126,
$$126 = 2 \times 3^2 \times 7$$

Example 2

$n = 153$. We have int$(\sqrt{n}) = 12$ and will scan p from 2 to 12.

$n_1 = 153$.
- $p = 2$: 2 does not divide 153.
- $p = 3$: Since $3 \mid 153$, we get $p_1 = 3$, $m_1 = 2$, $n_2 = n_1$ div 3^2
  $= 153$ div $9 = 17$.
- All numbers from 4 to 12 do not divide 17.

The scanning process is broken at $p = 13 > 12$.

Since $n_2 = 17 > 1$, we get $n_2 = 17$ as the largest prime factor of 153.

Moreover, we also get the prime factorization of 153,
$$153 = 3^2 \times 17$$

To enhance the efficiency of the algorithm we add the following features,
- Set the condition for the end of the process as $n = 1$ or $p >$ int$(\sqrt{n})$.
- If the given n is an odd number, then we scan only each odd number $p = 3, 5, 7, \ldots$
- If n is an even number then first, we compute $n = 2^m \times n_1$, n_1 is an odd number, then scan for the odd numbers $p = 3, 5, 7, \ldots$ Recall that the given n in the problem is odd.

```
Algorithm E3
Input: n = 60851475143 (odd number)
Output: p - the largest prime factor of n.
begin
  pmax ← 1;
  k ← 0;
  for p ← 3 to int(√n) step 2 do
    if (n = 1) then breakfor endif
    if (n mod p) = 0 then
        pmax ← p
        while ((n mod p) = 0) do n ← n div p endwhile
    endif
  endfor
  if (n > 1) then return n else return pmax endif;
endE3
```

Algorithm E3 needs $\text{int}(\sqrt{n})$ steps, each step needs maximum $\log n$ divisions, where $\log = \log_2$.

In the next programs we give function E3(n) to find the largest prime factor of any positive integer n. The type of parameter n in the function has 64 bits size. In general, an integer type of k bits has

minimum value $= -2^{k-1}$.

maximum value $= 2^{k-1}-1$.

Thus, the 64 bits integer has

minimum value $= -2^{63} = -9,223,372,036,854,775,808$.

maximum value $= 2^{63}-1 = 9,223,372,036,854,775,807$.

C++ Program

```
/**************************************
  Problem 3: Largest prime factor
            of 600851475143 ?
  Answer = 6857, Time = 0.02 sec.
**************************************/
  #include <iostream>
  #include <windows.h>
  #include <math.h>
```

```
using namespace std;

typedef unsigned long long Long;
// Long has size = 8 bytes = 64 bits

Long MN = 600851475143; // sqrt = 775146

int E3(Long n) {
  int s = int(sqrt((double) n));
  int p, pmax;
  p = 2; // case n is even
  if ((n % p) == 0) {
    pmax = p;
    while ((n % p) == 0) n /= p;
  }// if
  // n is odd
  for (p = 3; (n > 1) && (p <= s); p += 2) {
    if ((n % p) == 0) {
      pmax = p;
      while ((n % p) == 0) n /= p;
    } // if
  } // for
  return (n > 1) ? n : pmax;
} // E3

main() {
  cout << E3(MN);
  cout << "\n T H E    E N D";
  return 0;
}
```

Free Pascal Program

```
(*****************************************
  Problem 3: Largest prime factor
              of 600851475143 ?
  Answer = 6857, Time = 0.02 sec.
*****************************************)
type int = int64; // size = 8 bytes = 64 bits
var MN: int = 600851475143;//sqrt of n = 775146

function E3(n: int): int;
  var s, p, pmax: int;
begin
```

```
 p := 2; // case n is even
 if (n mod p) = 0 then
 begin
   pmax := p;
   while (n mod p = 0) do n := n div p;
 end;
 // n is odd
 s := round(sqrt(n));
 p := 3;
 while ((n > 1) and (p <= s)) do
 begin
   if ((n mod p) = 0) then
   begin
     pmax := p;
     while ((n mod p) = 0) do n := n div p;
   end; // if
   p := p + 2;
 end; // while
 if n > 1 then pmax := n;
 exit(pmax);
end; // E3

BEGIN
  writeln(E3(MN)); // 6857
  writeln(' T H E    E N D .');
  readln;
End.
```

Java Program

```
/*************************************
  Problem 3. Largest prime factor
          of 600851475143
  Answer = 6857, Time = 0.02 sec.
**************************************/
public class E3 {
  private long MN = 600851475143L;

  E3(){
    System.out.println(lagestPrimeFactor(MN));
    // 6857
  }

    private long lagestPrimeFactor(long n) {
```

```
    long p, pmax = 1;
    p = 2; // case n is even
    if ((n % p) == 0) {
      pmax = p;
      while ((n % p) == 0) n /= p;
    }
      long s = (long)Math.sqrt(n);
    // n is odd
    for (p = 3; (n > 1) && (p <= s); p += 2) {
      if (n % p == 0) {
        pmax = p;
        while ((n % p) == 0) n /= p;
      } // if
    } // for
    return (n > 1)? n : pmax;
  } // lagestPrimeFactor
} // class E3
```

Problem 4. Largest palindrome product

A palindromic number reads the same both ways. The largest palindrome made from the product of two 2-digit numbers is 9009, which is 91 times 99. Find the largest palindrome made from the product of two 3-digit numbers.

Algorithms

Let E4 be the largest palindrome made from the product of two 3-digit numbers. There are two versions for the problem solving, E4A and E4B.

E4A

Let n be a natural number. We define by n' the reversed-written number of n. For example, if $n = 1024$, then $n' = 4201$; if $n = 1200$, then $n' = 21$. A natural number n is a *palindrome* if and only if $n' = n$.

If n is a 3-digit natural number, then $100 \leq n \leq 999$. A natural and naive algorithm is computing product $c = ab$ for all numbers a and b from 999 down to 100, and then testing if $c = c'$ to get the maximum value of c.

Algorithm E4A
Input: minval = 100; maxval = 999;
Output: cmax = max {c | c = a×b, c = c', minval ≤ a, b ≤ maxval}
begin
cmax ← 0
for a ← maxval downto minval do
for b ← maxval downto minval do
c ← a × b;
if (c' = c) then
cmax ← max {c, cmax}
endif
endfor b
endfor a
return cmax
end E4A

To compute the reversed number n' of a given positive integer n, we get each digit of n from right (low position) to the left (high position) and append it to the right of n'. The next example shows how to find n' from the given $n = 1234$.

n	1	2	3	4	steps	n'	0			
	1	2	3		1		4			
	1	2			2		4	3		
	1				3		4	3	2	
	0				4		4	3	2	1

```
Algorithm Rev
Input: integer n ≥ 0
Output: r - reversed-written number of n.
         r = Rev(n) = n'
begin
  r ← 0
  while (n ≠ 0) do
        r ← r×10 + (n mod 10)
        n ← n div 10
  endwhile
  return r
end Rev
```

To enhance the efficiency of algorithm E4A, we add the following features:

- Since product $a \times b$ is commutative, we scan only for $b \le a$.

- Since subtraction is faster than multiplication, we replace multiplication $c = a(b-1)$ by $c = c-a$, where $c = ab$ is computed on the previous step.

- For each a, we scan $b = a$ down to minval and compute $c = ab$. If we get $c = c'$, then for all the next b, we have $ab < c$, hence we can break the loop at this point.

- If $c_i = a_ib_i$ and $c_i' = c_i$ for some $100 \leq a_i$, $b_i \leq 999$, then in the next step we have $a_{i+1} < a_i$, hence we may only scan b from a_i down to $b_i + 1$ to get $a_{i+1}b_{i+1} > a_ib_i$.

```
Algorithm E4A
Input: minval = 100; maxval = 999;
Output: cmax = max {c | c = a×b, c = c', minval ≤ a, b ≤ maxval}
begin
   cmax ← 0; limb ← minval;
   for a ← maxval downto minval do
       c = a×(a+1);
       for b ← a downto limb do
           c ← c − a; // c = ab
           if (c ≤ cmax) then breakforb endif;
           // c > cmax
           if (Rev(c) = c) then
               cmax = c ;
               limb ← b + 1;
               breakforb;
           endif
       endfor b
   endfor a
   return cmax
end E4A
```

E4B

(MathBlog https://www.mathblog.dk/project-euler-problem-4/)

Let x be a positive integer and x' be its reversed-written number. If we concatenate x' to x as two strings, then we get a palindrome, written as $x{:}x'$. For example, if $x = 102$, then $x{:}x' = 102{:}201 = 102201$, if $x = 820$, then $x{:}x' = 820{:}028 = 820028$.

The following algorithm, GetPal(x), returns the palindrome $x{:}x'$ from a given non-negative integer x.

```
Algorithm GetPal
Input: integer x ≥ 0
Output: palindrome y = x:x'
begin
    y ← x
    while (x ≠ 0) do
        y ← y×10 + (x mod 10)
        x ← x div 10
    endwhile
    return y
end GetPal
```

Now, for each 3-digit integer x we construct the palindrome $c = x{:}x'$ and test if c is a product of some a and b, $100 \leq a, b \leq 999$.

First, we need to find the start value, *astart* and the end value, *aend* for the scanning value a. The maximum palindrome is $c = x{:}x' = 999999$ generated by $x = 999$. If $a = b = 999$, then $a{\times}b = 999{\times}999 = 998001$, which is not a palindrome. Thus, the maximum palindrome is $c = 997799$, which is constructed by $x = 997$. We set *astart* = 997 and will find *aend*. By the commutative law of multiplication, we let $a \geq b$. This implies that $aend = \mathrm{int}(\sqrt{c})$.

```
Algorithm E4B
Input: minval = 100; maxval = 999.
Output: max {c | c = a×b, c = c', minval ≤ a, b ≤ maxval}
begin
    astart ← 997;
    for x ← astart down to 100 do
        c ← GetPal(x); // c = x:x'
        aend ← int(√c);
        for a ← astart down to aend do
            b ← c div a
            if (b > maxval) then breakfora endif
            if (a×b = c) then return c endif
        endfor a
    endfor x
end E4A
```

The next programs give values amax, bmax and palindrome cmax = amax × bmax for E4A version, and a, b and palindrome c = a × b for E4B version.

C++ Program

```
/*********************************************
  Problem 4. Largest palindrome product.
  Versions E4A, E14B
  Answer: 906609 = 913x993,Time = 0.09 sec.
**********************************************/
#include <iostream>
#include <windows.h>
#include <math.h>

using namespace std;

// n' = Rev(int n)
int Rev(int n) {
  int r = 0;
  while (n != 0) {
    r = r*10 + (n % 10);
    n /= 10;
  }
  return r;
} // Rev

void E4A() {
  int minval = 100;
  int maxval = 999;
  int a, b, c, amax, bmax, cmax;
  int limb;
  cmax = 1; limb = minval - 1;
  for (a = maxval; a >= minval; --a) {
    c = a*(a+1);
    for (b = a; b > limb; --b) {
      c -= a; // c is decreasing
      if (c <= cmax) break;  // forb
      // c > cmax
      if (Rev(c) == c) {
        cmax = c;
        amax = a;
```

```cpp
          bmax = b;
          limb = b;
          break; // for b
        } // if Rev
      } // for b
    } // for a
    cout << "\n E4A: " << cmax << " = "
         << amax << " * " << bmax;
  } // E4A

  // y = x:x'
  int GetPal(int x) {
    int y = x;
    while (x != 0) {
      y = y*10 + (x % 10);
      x /= 10;
    }
    return y;
  } // GetPal

  // See MathBlog
  // https://www.mathblog.dk/project-euler-problem-4/)
  void E4B() {
    int x, c, a, b, astart, aend;
    astart = 997;
    for (x = astart; x >= 100; --x) {
      c = GetPal(x); // c = xx'
      aend = int(sqrt(c));
      for (a = astart; a >= aend; --a) {
        b = c / a;
        if (b > astart) break; // for a
        if (a*b == c) {
          cout << "\n E4B: " << c << " = "
               << a << " * " << b;
          return;
        }// if
      } // for a
    }// for x
  } // E4B

  main() {
    E4A(); // 913*993 = 906609
    E4B(); // 913*993 = 906609
```

```
  //------------------------------
  cout << "\n T H E    E N D";
  return 0;
}
```

Free Pascal Program

```
(**********************************************
  Problem 4. Largest palindrome product
  Versions E4A, E14B
  Answer: 906609 = 913 x 993,Time = 0.09 sec.
**********************************************)

type int = longint;

// n' = Rev(int n)
function Rev(n: int): int;
  var r: int;
begin
  r := 0;
  while (n <> 0) do
  begin
    r := r*10 + (n mod 10);
    n := n div 10;
  end;
  exit(r);
end;

procedure E4A;
  var minval, maxval,
  a, b, c, amax, bmax, cmax,
  limb: int;
begin
  minval := 100;
  maxval := 999;
  cmax := 1; limb := minval;
  for a := maxval downto minval do
  begin
    c := a*(a+1);
    for b := a downto limb do
    begin
      c := c-a;
      if (c <= cmax) then break; // b
      // c > cmax
```

```
      if (Rev(c) = c) then
      begin
        cmax := c;
        amax := a;
        bmax := b;
        limb := b + 1;
        break;
      end; // if c
    end; // for b
  end; // for a
  writeln(' E4A: ', cmax, ' = ',
          amax, ' * ',  bmax);
end; // E4A

// y = x:x'
function GetPal(x: int) : int;
  var y: int;
begin
  y := x;
  while (x <> 0) do
  begin
    y := y*10 + (x mod 10);
    x := x div 10;
  end;
  exit(y);
end;

// See MathBlog
// https://www.mathblog.dk/project-euler-problem-4/)
procedure E4B;
  var x, c, a, b, astart, aend: int;
begin
  astart := 997;
  for x := astart downto 100 do
  begin
    c := GetPal(x); // c = xx'
    aend := round(sqrt(c));
    for a := astart downto aend do
    begin
      b := c div a;
      if (b > astart) then break; // for a
      if (a*b = c) then
      begin
        writeln(' E4B: ',c,' = ',a,' * ',b);
```

```
      exit;
     end;
    end; // for a
  end; // for x
end; // E4B

BEGIN
  E4A; // 913*993 = 906609
  E4B; // 913*993 = 906609
  //-----------------------------
  writeln(' T H E    E N D . ');
  readln;
END.
```

Java Program

```java
/*************************************************
    Problem 4. Largest palindrome product
    Answer: 99000099 = 9999x9901,Time=0.09 sec.
*************************************************/
public class E4 {
  E4(){
    E4A();
    E4B();
  }

  // n' = Rev(int n)
  private int Rev(int n) {
   int r = 0;
   while (n != 0) {
     r = r*10 + (n % 10);
     n /= 10;
   } // while
   return r;
   } // Rev

  private void E4A() {
   int minval = 100;
   int maxval = 999;
   int a, b, c, amax = 0, bmax = 0, cmax;
   int limb = minval + 1;
   cmax = 1;
   for (a = maxval; a >= minval; --a) {
     c = a*(a+1);
```

```
    for (b = a; b >= limb; --b) {
      c -= a;
      if (c <= cmax) break; //b
      // c > cmax
      if (Rev(c) == c){
          cmax = c;
          amax = a;
          bmax = b;
          limb = b + 1;
          break;
      } // if c
    } // for b
  } // for a
  System.out.println("\n E4A: "+cmax+" = "
                            +amax+" * "+bmax);
  } // E4A

  private void E4B() {
  // See MathBlog
  // https://www.mathblog.dk/project-euler-problem-4/)
   int x, c, a, b, astart, aend;
   astart = 997;
   for (x = astart; x >= 100; --x) {
    c = GetPal(x); // c = xx'
    aend = (int)Math.sqrt(c);
    for (a = astart; a >= aend; --a) {
    b = c / a;
    if (b > astart) break; // for a
    if (a*b == c) {
        System.out.println("\n E4B: "+c
                          +" = "+a+" * "+b);
        return;
    } // if
    } // for a
   }// for x
  } // E4B

  // y = x:x'
  private int GetPal(int x) {
   int y = x;
   while (x != 0) {
     y = y*10 + (x % 10);
     x /= 10;
   } // while
```

```
  return y;
  } // GetPal
} // class E4
```

Problem 5. Smallest multiple

2520 is the smallest number that can be divided by each of the numbers from 1 to 10 without any remainder.

What is the smallest positive number that is evenly divisible (divisible with no remainder) by all the numbers from 1 to 20?

Algorithm

The *greatest common divisor* of two integers a and b, which are not all zero, denoted by $\gcd(a, b)$ or (a, b), is the largest positive integer d that divides both a and b.

We extend the notion of the greatest common divisor to a set of arbitrary integers by the following properties:

Properties of gcd

for all integers $a, b, a_1, a_2, ..., a_n$

gcd1. $(a) = |a|$.

gcd2. $(a, 0) = (0, a) = |a|$.

gcd3. $(0, 0) = 0$ (accepted).

gcd4. $(a, b) = (b, a)$.

gcd5. $(a, b) = (|a|, |b|)$.

gcd6. $(a, b) = (a \bmod b, b)$.

gcd7. $(a, b) = (a - b, b)$.

gcd8. if $a \mid b$ then $(a, b) = |a|$.

gcd9. $(a_1, a_2, ..., a_n) = ((a_1, a_2, ..., a_{n-1}), a_n)$.

Examples

$(4, 12) = 4$.

$(15, 21, 7) = ((15, 21), 7) = (3, 7) = 1$.

Using gcd6, gcd4 and gcd2, we obtain $(49, 14) = (49 \bmod 14, 14) = (7, 14) = (14, 7) = (14 \bmod 7, 7) = (0, 7) = (7, 0) = 7$.

The last example above shows the process of computing gcd by the Euclid's algorithm:

a	b	r = a mod b
49	14	7
14	7	0
7	0	
	gcd(49, 14) = 7	

```
Algorithm gcd
Input: integers a, b.
Output: (a, b)
begin
  a ← |a|;  b ← |b|;
  while (b ≠ 0) do
        r ← a mod b;
        a ← b;
        b ← r;
  endwhile // b = 0
  return a
end gcd
```

The *least common multiple* of two non-zero integers a and b, denote by lcm(a, b) or [a, b], is the smallest positive integer m that is divisible by both a and b.

We extend the notion of the least common multiple to a set of arbitrary non-zero integers by the following properties:

Properties of lcm

for all non-zero integers a, b, a_1, a_2, ..., a_n

lcm1. $[a] = |a|$.

lcm2. $[a, 1] = [1, a] = |a|$.

lcm3. $[a, b] = [b, a]$.

lcm4. $[a, b] = [|a|, |b|]$.

lcm5. $[a, b] = ab$ div $(a, b) = a(b$ div $(a, b)) = (a$ div $(a, b))b$.

lcm6. If $a \mid b$ then $[a, b] = |b|$.

lcm7. $[a_1, a_2, ..., a_n] = [[a_1, a_2, ..., a_{n-1}], a_n]$.

Examples

$[4, 12] = 12$.

$[4, 6] = 12$.

$[4, 7] = 28$.

$[4, 6, 3] = [[4, 6], 3] = [12, 3] = 12$.

The request of the problem is

$[1, 2, 3, 4, 5, 6, 7, 8, 9, 10, 11, 12, 13, 14, 15, 16, 17, 18, 19, 20]$

Property lcm5 gives an algorithm for computing lcm.

Algorithm lcm
Input: integers $a, b, a \neq 0, b \neq 0$
Output: lcm(a, b)
begin
return (|a| div gcd(a,b)) × |b|;
end lcm

Note

In the algorithm lcm, if we write (a×b) div gcd(a,b), then the product a×b may be very large. Hence, we use division for the first, namely, we set (a div gcd(a,b)) × b.

Using properties lcm4 and lcm5, and the fact that lcm$(1, d) = d$ we can get an algorithm for computing lcm of a given sequence of integers.

```
Algorithm MultiLcm
Input: s - set of positive integers
Output: m = lcm(s)
begin
   m ← 1;
   for each number d in s do
        m ← lcm(m, d);
   endfor
   return m;
end MultiLcm
```

Consider the first n natural numbers, $n = 20$,

   $s = (1, 2, 3, 4, 5, 6, 7, 8, 9, 10, 11, 12, 13, 14, 15, 16, 17, 18, 19, 20)$

Any number d between 1 and (n div 2) divides $2d$. By property lcm6, if d divides m then we can remove d from s. We get,

   1, 2, 3, 4, 5, 6, 7, 8, 9, 10, 11, 12, 13, 14, 15, 16, 17, 18, 19, 20.

where underlined numbers are removed. Thus, the result is

   MultiLcm(s) = MultiLcm(11, 12, 13, 14, 15, 16, 17, 18, 19, 20)

In general, to compute lcm of the first n natural numbers, 1, 2, ..., n we simple call algorithm MultiLcm for numbers between (n div 2) +1 and n as follows

```
Algorithm MLcm
Input: integer n > 0
Output: d = MultiLcm(1, 2, ..., n)
begin
   m ← 1;
   for i ← (n div 2) + 1 to n do
      m ← i × (m div gcd(i, m));
   endfor
   return m;
end MLcm
```

C++ Program

```cpp
/*****************************************
  Problem 5. Smallest multiple
  Answer = 232792560, Time = 0.02 sec.
******************************************/
#include <iostream>
#include <windows.h>

using namespace std;

// Euclid
inline int Gcd(int a, int b) {
  int r;
  while(b != 0) {
    r = a % b;
    a = b;
    b = r;
  } // while
  return a;
}// Gcd

int MLcm(int n) {
  int m = 1;
  for (int i = n/2+1; i <= n; ++i)
    m = i*(m/Gcd(i,m));
  return m;
} // MLcm

main() {
  cout << endl << MLcm(20); // 232792560
  cout << "\n T H E    E N D";
  return 0;
}
```

Free Pascal Program

```pascal
(*****************************************
  Problem 5. Smallest multiple
  Answer = 232792560, Time = 0.02 sec.
******************************************)

type int = longint;
// Euclid
```

```
function Gcd(a, b: int): int;
  var r: int;
begin
  while(b <> 0) do
  begin
    r := a mod b;
    a := b;
    b := r;
  end; // while
  exit(a);
end; // Gcd

function MLcm(n: int): int;
  var i, m: int;
begin
  m := 1;
  for i := n div 2 + 1 to n do
    m := i*(m div Gcd(i, m));
  exit(m);
end; // MLcm

BEGIN
  writeln(MLcm(20)); // 232792560
  writeln(' T H E    E N D .');
  readln;
END.
```

Java Program

```
/*********************************************
  Problem 5. Smallest multiple
  Answer = 232792560, Time = 0.02 sec.
*********************************************/

public class E5 {
  E5() {
    System.out.println(MLcm(20));
  }

   private int MLcm(int n) {
    int m = 1;
    for (int i = n/2 + 1; i <= n; ++i)
      m = i*(m / Gcd(i,m));
    return m;
```

```
    } // MLcm

    // Euclid
    private int Gcd(int a, int b) {
     int r = 0;
     while (b != 0){
       r = a % b;
       a = b;
       b = r;
     } // while
     return a;
     } // Gcd
} // class E5
```

50 , 10

r = 0

r = 50 % 10

= 5

a = 10

b = 5

r =

50 | 30

r = 20

a = 30

b = 20

r = 10

a = 20

b = 10

r = 0

a = 10

b = 0

10

Problem 6. Sum square difference

The sum of the squares of the first ten natural numbers is $1^2 + 2^2 + \ldots + 10^2 = 385$.

The square of the sum of the first ten natural numbers is $(1 + 2 + \ldots + 10)^2 = 55^2 = 3025$.

Hence the difference between the sum of the squares of the first ten natural numbers and the square of the sum is $3025 - 385 = 2640$.

Find the difference between the sum of the squares of the first one hundred natural numbers and the square of the sum.

Understanding

Given a natural number $n > 0$. Denote by

$\quad G(n) = 1 + 2 + \ldots + n,$

$\quad S_1(n) = 1^2 + 2^2 + \ldots + n^2$, and

$\quad S_2(n) = (1 + 2 + \ldots + n)^2 = G^2(n).$

The request of the problem is finding the difference $D = S_2(100) - S_1(100)$.

Algorithm

It is well-known that,

$$G(n) = 1 + 2 + \cdots + n = \frac{n(n+1)}{2} \qquad (Gauss)$$

and

$$S_1 = 1^2 + 2^2 + \cdots + n^2 = \frac{n(n+1)(2n+1)}{6} =$$

$$= \frac{n(n+1)}{2} \times \frac{2n+1}{3} = G(n) \times \frac{2n+1}{3}$$

Hence,

$$D(n) = S_2(n) - S_1(n) =$$

$$= G^2(n) - G(n) \times \frac{n + n + 1}{3} \qquad (6.1)$$

which needs three multiplications, two divisions, three additions, and one subtraction.

Comment

Of course, you can compute $D(n)$ by the following formula, which is realized in the Java program below,

$$D(n) = \frac{n^2(n+1)^2}{4} - \frac{n(n+1)(2n+1)}{6} =$$

$$= \frac{n(n+1)(3n^2 - n - 2)}{12} \qquad (6.2)$$

and needs four multiplications, one division, one addition, and two subtractions. Thus, the formulas (6.2) and (6.1) can be seen of the same complexity.

C++ Program

```
/ * * * * * * * * * * * * * * * * * * * * * * * * * * * * * * * * * * * * * * *
  Problem 6. Sum square difference
   Answer = 25164150, Time = 0.02 sec.
* * * * * * * * * * * * * * * * * * * * * * * * * * * * * * * * * * * * * * */
#include <iostream>

using namespace std;

int E6() {
  int n = 100;
  int n1 = n+1;
  int G = (n * n1)/2;
  int S1 = (G*(n + n1)) / 3;
  return G*G - S1;
} // E6

main() {
  cout << E6();    // 25164150
  cout << "\n T H E    E N D .";
  return 0;
}
```

Free Pascal Program

```
(**************************************
  Problem 6. Sum square difference
  Result: 25164150, Time = 0.02 sec.
 **************************************)
type int = longint;

function E6: int;
  var n,n1, G, S1: int;
begin
  n := 100;
  n1:= n+1;
  G := (n*n1) div 2;
  S1 := G*(n + n1) div 3;
  exit(G*G - S1);
end;

BEGIN
  writeln(E6); // 25164150
  writeln(' T H E    E N D . ');
  readln;
END.
```

Java Program

```
/**************************************
  Problem 6. Sum square difference
  Answer = 25164150, Time = 0.02 sec.
 **************************************/
public class E6 {
  E6(){
    int n = 100;
    int nn = n*n;
    System.out.println(n*(n+1)*(3*nn-n-2)/12);
    // 25164150
  } // E6
} // class E6
```

Problem 7. 10001st prime

By listing the first six prime numbers: 2, 3, 5, 7, 11, and 13, we can see that the 6th prime is 13.

What is the 10001st prime number?

Algorithm

A natural number $n > 1$ is a *prime* if and only if it has no prime factors $\leq \sqrt{n}$. We will generate a sequence of the first 10001 primes and write them to an array $p[]$ as follow.

Step 1. *Initialize*: Set $p[1] = 2$ and $p[2] = 3$ - the first two primes.

Step 2. *Loop*: Let $p = (p[1], p[2], ..., p[k])$, $k \geq 2$ be the first k generated primes, and $p[n]$ be the first number in p that $(p[n])^2 > p[k]$. Note that all primes greater than 2 are odd numbers. For all odd integer x, $p[k]+2 \leq x < (p[n])^2$, if x has a divisor d such that $3 \leq d < p[n]$, then x is a composite. If not, then x is a new prime greater than $p[k]$, and we append x to p. If $k = 10001$ then we return $p[k]$ and stop the algorithm, otherwise we repeat the loop.

The next example illustrates the approach.

Example

Let $k = 10$, $n = 4$ and $p[1...10] = (2, 3, 5, \underline{7}, 11, 13, 17, 19, 23, 29)$ be the first ten generated primes. We have, $p[n] = p[4] = 7$, $(p[n])^2 = 7 \times 7 = 49 > 29 = p[10]$. For each odd number x from 29+2 = 31 to 49−2 = 47, we test if x is a multiple of 3 or 5. If not then we append them to p.

$x = 31$. Since both 3 and 5 do not divide 31, 31 is a new prime. Append 31 to p: $p[11] = \mathbf{31}$;

$x = 33$. Since $3 \mid 33$, ignore;

$x = 35$. Since $5 \mid 35$, ignore;

$x = 37$. Since both 3 and 5 do not divide 37. Append 37 to p: $p[12] = \mathbf{37}$;

$x = 39$. Since $3 \mid 39$, ignore;

$x = 41$. Since both 3, 5 do not divide 41. Append 41 to p: $p[13] = \mathbf{41}$;

$x = 43$. Since both 3, 5 do not divide 43. Append 43 to p: $p[14] =$ **43**;

$x = 45$. Since 5 | 45, ignore;

$x = 47$. Since both 3, 5 do not divide 47. Append 47 to p: $p[15] =$ **47**.

Finally, we get $k = 15$, and $p[1\ldots15] = (2, 3, 5, 7, 11, 13, 17, 19, 23, 29,$ **31**, **37**, **41**, **43**, **47**$)$, where the newly added primes are bold printed. Now, the process is repeated for $n = 5$, $k = 15$ and testing for all odd numbers between $(p[n\text{-}1])^2 + 2 = 49+2 = 51$ and $(p[n])^2 - 2 = 121 - 2 = 119$ if they are multiples of 3, 5, or 7 (all odd primes below $p[n]$).

Of course, you can start with $p[1]=2$; $p[2]=3$ and $n=k=2$, but it will be better if we begin with the first ten primes,

```
int p[MN] = {0,2,3,5,7,11,13,17,19,23,29};
k = 10; n = 4;
//(p[n])²=(p[4])²=7×7=49 > 29=p[10]=p[k]
```

Note

In C++ and Java, the first index of the array is 0, hence we set a[0]=0 and begin with the index 1, ignoring a[0].

C++ Program

```
/**********************************
  Problem 7. 10001st prime
  Answer = 104743, Time = 0.02 sec.
***********************************/
#include <iostream>

const int MN = 10002;

using namespace std;

// first 10 primes
int p[MN]={0,2,3,5,7,11,13,17,19,23,29};

// x is prime iff x has no factor p[2]...p[n-1]
// Since x is odd we do not test

bool Prime(int n, int x) {
    for (int i = 2; i < n; ++i)
```

```
    if ((x % p[i]) == 0) return false;
 return true;
 } // Prime

 int E7() {
  int  x, n, k, m;
  k = 10;  // p[k] is the last prime
           // of started sequence
  n = 3;
  // p[n]=5, p[n+1]=p[4]=7, p[n+1]*p[n+1]>p[k]
  m = p[k];
  while (true) {
    x = m + 2;
    ++n;
    m = p[n]*p[n];
    // Scan from p[k]+2 to m
    for (; x < m; x += 2)
    if (Prime(n, x)) {
      p[++k] = x;
      if (k == 10001) return x;
    } // if
  } // while
 } // E7

 main() {
    cout << "    " << E7();
    // ----------------------------------
    cout << "\n T H E    E N D";
    return 0;
 }
```

Free Pascal Program

```
 (*************************************
    Problem 7. 10001st prime
    Answer = 104743, Time = 0.02 sec.
 *************************************)

 const MN = 10001;

 type int = longint;

var
 // first 10 primes
```

```
  p: array[1..MN] of int;
  // x is prime iff x has no factor p[2]…p[n-1]
  // x is odd

function Prime(n, x: int): boolean;
  var i: int;
begin
  for i := 2 to n-1 do
    if ((x mod p[i]) = 0) then exit(false);
  exit(true);
end; // Prime

function E7: int;
  var x, n, k, m : int;
begin
  p[1] := 2; p[2] := 3; p[3] := 5; p[4] := 7;
  p[5] := 11; p[6] := 13; p[7] := 17; p[8] := 19;
  p[9] := 23; p[10] := 29;
  k := 10;
  // p[k] is the last prime in started sequence
  n := 3;
  // p[n]=5, p[n+1]=p[4]=7, p[n+1]*p[n+1] > p[k]
  m := p[k];
  while (true) do
  begin
    x := m+2;
    inc(n);
    m := p[n]*p[n];
    // Scan to m
    while (x < m) do
    begin
      if (Prime(n, x)) then
      begin
        inc(k); p[k] := x;
        if (k = 10001) then exit(x);
      end; // if
      x := x + 2;
    end; // while x
  end; // while true
end; // E7

BEGIN
  writeln('    ', E7);
  // ----------------------------------
```

```
  writeln(' T H E    E N D .');
  readln;
END.
```

Java Program

```
/*********************************
  Problem 7. 10001st prime
  104743, Time = 0.02 sec.
*********************************/
public class E7 {
  private int MN = 10002;
  private int [] p = new int[MN];

  E7(){
    System.out.println(Extend());// 104743
  }

   private int Extend() {
    int  x, n, k, m;
    p[0]=0; p[1]=2; p[2]=3; p[3]=5; p[4]=7;
    p[5]=11; p[6]=13; p[7]=17;p[8]=19;
    p[9]=23; p[10]=29;
    k = 10;
    //p[k] is the last prime of started sequence
    n = 3;
    // p[n]=5, p[k]=p[4]=7, p[n+1]*p[n+1] > p[k]
    m = p[k];
    while (true) {
      x = m + 2;
      ++n;
      m = p[n]*p[n];
      // Scan from p[k]+2 to m
      for (; x < m; x += 2)
      if (Prime(n, x)) {
          p[++k] = x;
          if (k == 10001) return x;
      } // if
    } // while
  } // Extend

  // x is prime iff x has no factor p[2]…p[n]
  // x is odd
```

```
  private boolean Prime(int n, int x) {
    for (int i = 2; i < n; ++i)
      if ((x % p[i]) == 0) return false;
   return true;
  }
} // class E7
```

Comment

The Sieve of Eratosthenes

Since multiplication is a faster operation than division, Greek mathematician Eratosthenes had the idea of organizing the computation in the form of the well-known sieve. We illustrate its use in Table 7.1 by finding all primes less than 100.

1	2	3	4	5	6	7	8	9	10
11	12	13	14	15	16	17	18	19	20
21	22	23	24	25	26	27	28	29	30
31	32	33	34	35	36	37	38	39	40
41	42	43	44	45	46	47	48	49	50
51	52	53	54	55	56	57	58	59	60
61	62	63	64	65	66	67	68	69	70
71	72	73	74	75	76	77	78	79	80
81	82	83	84	85	86	87	88	89	90
91	92	93	94	95	96	97	98	99	100

Table 7.1 *The Sieve of Eratosthenes up to 100.*
(The deleted numbers are in colored cells.
All the rest numbers are primes)

> **The lecture of Eratosthenes**
>
> Dear my students,
> Let's find out all primes below 100.
> Step 1. Write down 1 to 100 to your clay board.
> You have all undeleted numbers from 1 to 100.
> Step 2. Delete 1, because 1 is not a prime nor a compose. 1 is a special number.
> Step 3. Find the next undeleted number i. It is a new prime.
> Step 4. If $i > 10$ then you stop the work. All undeleted numbers on your board are primes.
> If $i \leq 10$ then you do Step 5.
> Step 5. Delete all multiples of i from i^2 to 100.
> Step 6. Repeat Step 3.

Eratosthenes
276 - 194 B.C.E.

Now we give a version of algorithm Sieve of Eratosthenes for any integer $n > 1$.

> **Algorithm Sieve**
>
> Input: Integer n > 1
> Output: All primes ≤ n.
> begin
>   Write 1, 2, ..., n;
>   Delete 1;
>   for i ← 2 to int($\sqrt{n}$) do
>   if (i is undeleted) then
>   for j ← i to (n div j) do
>   delete I × j
>   endfor j
>   endif
>   endfor i
>   return all undeleted numbers;
> endSieve

To apply Sieve(n) to the problem, we need to estimate the range of n. Denote by $\pi(n)$ the number of primes below a given natural number n.

From number theory, we know that $\pi(n)$ is asymptotic to $n / \log n$, which is denoted as $\pi(n) \approx \dfrac{n}{\log n}$

(*Crandall, Richard*, Pomerance, Carl (2005), *Prime Numbers: A Computational Perspective* (2nd ed.), Springer, p. 121, ISBN 9780387252827.)

In the other hand, $\log n$ (with base 2) is the number of bits representing n. If we take $\log n = 12$ then we have

$$n \approx \pi(n) \times \log n = 10001 \times 12 \approx 120000$$

Algorithm E7B
Input: 10001
Output: 10001st prime
begin
Sieve(120000);
$c \leftarrow 0$;
for each prime p in sieve do
$c \leftarrow c + 1$;
if (c = 10001) then return p endif;
endfor
endE7B

We use a bit sequence p to indicate each number i in the sieve is prime ($p[i] = 1$) or not ($p[i] = 0$). Some operators of the bitset type are given in table 7.2.

bitset in C++ bit value: `0,1`	BitSet in Java bit value: `false,true`	Comment
`#include <bitset>`	`import java.util.BitSet;`	Using library `bitset/Bitset`
`bitset<20> p;`	`BitSet p = new BitSet(20);` `// p[i]=false,0 ≤ i< 20`	Create bitset variable p with size 20, `p[0],...,p[19]`
`p.set();`	`p.set(0,20);`	Set all p[i]=1/true, $0 \le i < 20$
`p[i]`	`p.get(i)`	Return the value `0`/`falle` or `1`/`true` of p[i]
`p.set(i)`	`p.set(i)`	Set p[i] = `1`/`true`
`p.reset(i)`	`p.clear(i)`	Set p[i] = `0`/`false`

Table 7.2 Bitset operators in C++ and Java

C++ Program

```
/*********************************
  Problem 7. 10001st prime
  Version E7B
  Answer = 104743, Time = 0.04 sec.
*************************************/
#include <iostream>
#include <cmath>
#include <bitset>

const int MN = 10001*12;

using namespace std;

bitset<MN> p; // sieve

// Sieve of Eratosthenes
void Sieve() {
  int s = (int)sqrt(MN);
  p.set();
  for (int i = 2; i <= s; ++i)
    if (p[i])
      for (int j = i*i; j <= MN; j += i)
      p[j] = 0;
} // Sieve

int E7B() {
  Sieve();
  int c = 0;
  for (int i = 2; i <= MN; ++i)
    if (p[i]) {
      ++c;
      if (c == 10001) return i;
    } // if
} // E7B

main() {
  cout << "     " << E7B(); // 104743
  // ----------------------------------
  cout << "\n T H E    E N D";
  return 0;
}
```

Free Pascal Program

```
(***************************************
  Problem 7. 10001st prime
   Version E7B
   Answer = 104743, Time = 0.04 sec.
***************************************)

const MN = 12*10001; NL = #13#10; // new line
type int = longint;
var p: array[1..MN] of boolean;

// Sieve of Eratosthenes
procedure Sieve;
  var i, j, s: int;
begin
  s := round(sqrt(MN));
  fillchar(p, sizeof(p), true); // all true
  for i := 2 to s do
    if p[i] then
    begin
      j := i*i;
      while j <= MN do
      begin
        p[j] := false;
        j := j + i;
      end; // while
    end; // if
end; // Sieve

function E7B: int;
  var c, i: int;
begin
  Sieve;
  c := 0;
  for i := 2 to MN do
    if p[i] then
    begin
      inc(c);
      if c = 10001 then exit(i);
    end; // if
end; // E7B

BEGIN
```

```
  writeln(E7B);
  readln;
END.
```

Java Program

```java
/**********************************
  Problem 7. 10001st prime
  Version E7B
  Answer = 104743, Time = 0.04 sec.
**********************************/
import java.util.BitSet;
public class E7 {
  private int MN = 10001*12;
  private BitSet p = new BitSet(MN);
  private boolean PRIME = false;
  E7() {
    System.out.println(E7B());
  } // E7B

   // All primes <= n
   private void Sieve(){
    p.clear();
    int sq = (int)Math.sqrt(MN);
    for(int i = 2; i <= sq; ++i) {
      if (p.get(i) == PRIME) {
        for (int j = i*i; j <= MN ; j += i)
            p.set(j);
      } // if
    } // for i
   }// Sieve

   int E7B() {
    Sieve();
    int c = 0;
    for (int i = 2; i <= MN; ++i)
      if (p.get(i) == PRIME) {
        ++c;
        if (c == 10001) return i;
      } // if p
    return 0;
   } // E7B
} // class E7
```

Problem 8. Largest product in a series

The four adjacent digits in the 1000-digit number that have the greatest product are $9 \times 9 \times 8 \times 9 = 5832$.

```
73167176531330624919225119674426574742355349194934
96983520312774506326239578318016984801869478851843
85861560789112949495459501737958331952853208805511
12540698747158523863050715693290963295227443043557
66896648950445244523161731856403098711121722383113
62229893423380308135336276614282806444486645238749
30358907296290491560440772390713810515859307960866
70172427121883998797908792274921901699720888093776
65727333001053367881220235421809751254540594752243
52584907711670556013604839586446706324415722155397
53697817977784617406495514929086256932197846862248 2
83972241375657056057490261407972968652414535100474
8216637048440319989000889524345065854122758866688 1
16427171479924442928230863465674813919123162824586
17866458359124566529476545682848912883142607690042
24219022671055626321111109370544217506941658960408
07198403850962455444362981230987879927244284909188
84580156166097919133875499200524063689912560717606
05886116467109405077541002256983155200055935729725
71636269561882670428252483600823257530420752963450
```

Find the thirteen adjacent digits in the 1000-digit number that have the greatest product. What is the value of this product?

Algorithm

If the input is written in the two-dimensional string ss with 20 lines and 50 digits per line, then it is easy to transform ss to a string s. Now consider

$$s = s_0 s_1 \ldots s_{999}$$

as a 1000-digit number.

For a given natural number $k \geq 1$, denote by E8(k), the *greatest product of the k-adjacent digits* in s. The answer to the problem will be E8(13). We denote by

- $s[i, j] = s_i s_{i+1} \ldots s_j$, $i \leq j$ a *segment* in s. We call $s[i, j]$ *a pure segment* of s, if $s[d] \neq$ '0' for all d, $i \leq d \leq j$.
- $\#(s[i, j]) = j - i + 1$, $i \leq j$ the *number of digits* in segment $s[i, j]$.
- $P(i, j) = s[i] \times s[i+1] \times \ldots \times s[j]$ the *product of digits* of segment $s[i, j]$.

Examples

If s is given in the problem, and $k = 5$, then,

$s[0, 4] =$ "73167", and it is a pure segment of s.

$\#(s[0, 4]) = 5$.

$P(0, 4) = 7 \times 3 \times 1 \times 6 \times 7 = 882$.

$s[54, 58] =$ "35203", and it is not a pure segment of s, since $s[57] =$ '0'.

$P(54, 58) = 3 \times 5 \times 2 \times \underline{0} \times 3 = \underline{0}$.

The *window-sliding* technique may be used for computing E8(k).

Given an integer $k \geq 1$. A *window* is a *pure segment* $s[l, r]$ with the length k. If $s[l, r]$ is a window, then l is called its *left door*, r is called its *right door*, and $P(l, r)$ is called its *product*.

Let $g = s[i, j]$ be a pure segment with the length $j - i + 1 \geq k$. If $w = s[l, r]$ is a window in g, $r < j$, and $t = P(l, r)$ is its product, then to compute the product u of the next window $s[l+1, r+1]$ in $s[i, j]$ we need only do one division and one multiplication, namely,

$$u = (t \text{ div } s[l]) \times s[r+1]$$

In this case, we say that window w *slides* to the right by *shrinking its left door* and *expanding its right door*.

Thus, to compute the *greatest product* of k-adjacent digits, GP, in a pure segment $s[i, j]$, $j - i + 1 \geq k$, we move the window $s[l, r]$ from position $l = i$ to the right and get the maximum value of products at each step.

$$GP(i, j) = \max \{P(l, l+k-1) \mid i \le l \le j-k+1\}$$

If there is some zero in segment $s[i, j]$ then $P(i, j) = 0$. Therefore, we will compute the products only of pure segments in s. Let $z = (z_1, z_2, \ldots, z_u)$, $z_1 < z_2 < \ldots < z_u$ be all positions, where $s[z_m] = $ '0', $1 \le m \le u$. Then, all segments between those zero points, namely, all segments $s[z_m+1, z_{m+1}-1]$, $1 \le m < u$ are pure, and they are candidates for computing GP if their length $\ge k$. For the convenience of computing, we add to the z two boundaries, $z_0 = -1$ and $z_{u+1} = $ length$(s) = 1000$.

The results of the problem are $s[i, i+12]$ and E8(13) for some i, $0 \le i \le$ length$(s) - 13$.

Note

$D' = $ {'0', '1', $\ldots$, '9'} is the set of digit-characters, while $D = $ {0, 1, $\ldots$, 9} is the set of digits. The elements of the sets D' and D have different (ASCII) codes. To convert a digit-character $s[i]$ in D' to corresponding element d in D we use the following rules,

- In C++

```
d = s[i] - '0';
```
- In Pascal:

```
d := ord(s[i]) - ord('0');
```
- In Java

```
d = s.charAt(i) - '0';
```

C++ Program

```
/************************************************
   Problem 8. Largest product in a series
   Aswere: Product = 23514624000,
   Time = 0.02 sec.
   Start at position 197,
   Segment = "5576689664895"
*************************************************/
#include <iostream>

using namespace std;

typedef unsigned long long Long;
```

```
const int LEN = 1000;

int imax;
// The beginning index of the resulting segment
Long pmax; // The largest product

string ss[20]  = {
"73167176531330624919225119674426574742355349194934",
"96983520312774506326239578318016984801869478851843",
"85861560789112949495459501737958331952853208805511",
"12540698747158523863050715693290963295227443043557",
"66896648950445244523161731856403098711121722383113",
"62229893423380308135336276614282806444486645238749",
"30358907296290491560440772390713810515859307960866",
"70172427121883998797908792274921901699720888093776",
"65727333001053367881220235421809751254540594752243",
"52584907711670556013604839586446706324415722155397",
"53697817977846174069551492908625693219784686224825",
"83972241375657056057490261407972968652414535100474",
"82166370484403199890008895243450658541227588666881",
"16427171479924442928230863465674813919123162824586",
"17866458359124566529476545682848912883142607690042",
"24219022671055626321111109370544217506941658960408",
"07198403850962455444362981230987879927244284909188",
"84580156166097919133875499200524063689912560717606",
"05886116467109405077541002256983155200055935729725",
"71636269561882670428252483600823257530420752963450"};

string s;

// convert s[i] to digit number
inline int Num(int i) { return s[i]-'0'; }

// largest product in pure segment s[a, b]
void Segment(int a, int b, int k){
  int i;
  Long p = 1;
  // The first window s[l, r] length = k
  int l = a;
  int r = l+k-1;
  for (i = 1; i <= r; ++i) p *= Num(i);// product
  if (p > pmax) {
    pmax = p;
```

```
    imax = l; // Position, where get pmax
  }
  b = b - k + 1; // right limit of left door l
  for (; l <= b; ++l, ++r) {
    p = (p/Num(l)) * Num(r+1);// product of next window
    if (p > pmax) {
      pmax = p;
      imax = l+1;
    }// if
  } // for
} // Segment

// Find the next position j > i, s[j] = 0
int NextZero(int i) {
  for (i = i+1; i < LEN; ++i)
    if (s[i] == '0') return i;
  return LEN;
} // NextZero

void E8(int k) {
  int i;
  // Init
  // copy ss to s
  s = "";
  for (i = 0; i < 20; ++i) s += ss[i];
  pmax = 0;
  imax = -1;
  int z1, z2; // s[z1, z2] is a pure segment
  z1 = -1;
  while(true) {
    z2 = NextZero(z1);
    if (z2 - z1 - 1 >= k)
      Segment(z1+1, z2-1, k);
    if (z2 == LEN) break;
    z1 = z2;
  } // while
  cout << "\n Max Product = " << pmax;
  cout << "\n Start at " << imax;
  cout << "\n Segment: ";
  for (int i = 0; i < k; ++i)
   cout << s[imax+i];
} // E8

main() {
```

```
   E8(13);  // 23514624000
   cout << "\n T H E     E.N D. ";
   return 0;
}
```

Free Pascal Program

```
(*************************************************
   Problem 8. Largest product in a series
   Answer: Product = 23514624000,
      Time = 0.02 sec.
   Start at position 197,
   Segment = '5576689664895'
*************************************************)
type int = integer;
const LEN = 1000; NL = #13#10;
s: PChar =
'7316717653133062491922511967442657474235534919934'+
'9698352031277450632623957831801698480186947885184'+
'8586156078911294949545950173795833195285320880551'+
'1254069874715852386305071569329096329522744304355'+
'6689966489504452445231617318564030987111217223831'+
'6222989342338030813533627661428280644448664523874'+
'3035890729629049156044077239071381051585930796086'+
'7017242712188399879790879227492190169972088809377'+
'6572733300105336788122023542180975125454059475224'+
'5258490771167055601360483958644670632441572215539'+
'5369781797784617406495514929086256932197846862248'+
'8397224137565705605749026140797296865241453510047'+
'8216637048440319989000889524345065854122758866688'+
'1642717147992444292823086346567481391912316282458'+
'1786645835912456652947654568284891288314260769004'+
'2421902267105562632111110937054421750694165896040'+
'0719840385096245544436298123098787992724428490918'+
'8458015616609791913387549920052406368991256071760'+
'6058861164671094050775410022569831552000559357297'+
'7163626956188267042825248360082325753042075296345'+
'0';
var
   pmax: int64;
   imax: int;

// convert s[i] to digit
function Num(i: int): int;
begin
```

```
  exit(Ord(s[i]) - Ord('0'));
end; // Num

// largest product in a segment s[a, b]
procedure Segment(a, b, k: int);
  var  p: int64;
  l, r, i: int;
begin
  // The first window s[l, r] length = k
  l := a;
  r := l+k-1;
  p := 1;
  // Product
  for i := l to r do p := p * Num(i);
  if (p > pmax) then
  begin
    pmax := p;
    imax := l; // Position, where get pmax
  end;
  b := b - k + 1; // right limit of left door l
  for l := l to b do
  begin
    p := (p div Num(l)) * Num(r+1);
    // product of next window
    if (p > pmax) then
    begin
        pmax := p;
        imax := l+1;
    end; // if
    inc(r);
  end; // for
end; // Segment

// Find the next position j > i, s[j] = 0
function NextZero(i: int): int;
begin
  for i := i+1 to LEN-1 do
  if (s[i] = '0') then exit(i);
  exit(LEN);
end; // NextZero

procedure E8(k: int);
  var i: int;
  z1, z2: int;
```

```
begin
   // Init
   pmax := 0;
   imax := 0;
   z1 := -1;
   while (true) do
   begin
     z2 := NextZero(z1);
     if (z2 - z1 - 1 >= k) then
       Segment(z1+1, z2-1, k);
     if (z2 = LEN) then break;
     z1 := z2;
   end; // while
   writeln(NL, ' Product = ', pmax);
   writeln(' Start at ', imax);
   write(' Segment: ');
   for i := imax to imax+k-1 do
    write(s[i]);
end; // E8

BEGIN
  E8(13); // 23514624000
  writeln(NL,' T H E    E N D. ');
  readln;
END.
```

Note

Pchar is the new string type of Free Pascal with starting index 0 and the length can be large than 255.

Java Program

In Java version, the 1000-digit number is given as the sum of strings.

```
/*********************************************
   Problem 8. Largest product in a series
   Answer: Product = 23514624000,
      Time = 0.02 sec.
   Start at position 197,
   Segment = "5576689664895"
*********************************************/
public class E8 {
private String s =
```

```
"7316717653133062491922511967442657474235534919493 4" +
"9698352031277450632623957831801698480186947885184 3" +
"8586156078911294949545950173795833195285320880551 1" +
"1254069874715852386305071569329096329522744304355 7" +
"6689664895044524452316173185640309871112172238311 3" +
"6222989342338030813533627661428280644448664523874 9" +
"3035890729629049156044077239071381051585930796086 6" +
"7017242712188399879790879227492190169972088809377 6" +
"6572733300105336788122023542180975125454059475224 3" +
"5258490771167055601360483958644670632441572215539 7" +
"5369781797784617406495514929086256932197846862248 2" +
"8397224137565705605749026140797296865241453510047 4" +
"8216637048440319989000889524345065854122758866688 1" +
"1642717147992444292823086346567481391912316282458 6" +
"1786645835912456652947654568284891288314260769004 2" +
"2421902267105562632111110937054421750694165896040 8" +
"0719840385096245544436298123098787992724428490918 8" +
"8458015616609791913387549920052406368991256071760 6" +
"0588611646710940507754100225698315520005593572972 5" +
"7163626956188267042825248360082325753042075296345 0";

private int LEN = 1000;
private long pmax = 0;
private int imax = -1;

E8() {
  Run(13); //23514624000
}

private void Run(int k) {
   int i;
   // Init
   pmax = 0;
   imax = -1;
   int z1, z2; // s[z1, z2] is a pure segment
   z1 = -1;
   while(true) {
     z2 = NextZero(z1);
     if (z2 - z1 - 1 >= k)
        Segment(z1+1, z2-1, k);
     if (z2 == LEN) break;
      z1 = z2;
   } // while
  System.out.println("\n Max Product = "+pmax);
```

```java
    System.out.println("\n Start at "+imax);
    System.out.print("\n Segment: ");
    for (i = 0; i < k; ++i)
      System.out.print(s.charAt(imax+i));
  } // Run

  // convert s[i] to digit
  private int Num(int i) { return s.charAt(i)-'0'; }

  // largest product in a segment s[d, c]
  private  void Segment(int z1, int z2, int k){
    int i;
    long p = (long) 1;
    // The first window s[l, r] length = k
    int l = z1;
    int r = l+k-1;
    for (i = l; i <= r; ++i) p *= Num(i);// product
    if (p > pmax) {
      pmax = p;
      imax = l; // Position, where get pmax
    }
    z2 = z2 - k + 1; // right limit of left door l
    for (; l <= z2; ++l, ++r) {
      p = (p/Num(l)) * Num(r+1);
      // product of the next window
      if (p > pmax) {
        pmax = p;
        imax = l+1;
      }// if
    } // for
  } // Segment

  // Find the next position j > i, s[j] = 0
  private int NextZero(int i) {
   for (i = i+1; i < LEN; ++i)
     if (s.charAt(i) == '0') return i;
   return LEN;
  } // Nextzero
} // class E8
```

Problem 9. Special Pythagorean triplet

A Pythagorean triplet is a set of three positive integers (a, b, c), for which, $a^2 + b^2 = c^2$. For example, $3^2 + 4^2 = 5^2$ $(9 + 16 = 25)$.

There exists exactly one Pythagorean triplet for which $a + b + c = 1000$. Find the product abc.

Algorithm

For

any Pythagorean triplet $p = (a, b, c)$:

- ☞ *i.* There are no two equal numbers in p. Indeed, we have, $a^2 + b^2$ $= c^2$. If $a = b$, then $c = a\sqrt{2}$ is an irrational number, but not integer. If $a = c$ then $b = 0$, if $b = c$ then $a = 0$, while a and b are positive integers. It is clear that $c > a$, and $c > b$. So, we can assume that $0 < a < b < c$.

- ☞ *ii.* For any integer $k \geq 1$, (ka, kb, kc) is also a Pythagorean triplet. This is because, $(ka)^2 + (kb)^2 = k^2(a^2+b^2) = (kc)^2$. Thus, we will consider only such Pythagorean triplets, that $\gcd(a, b, c) = 1$. These triplets are called *primitive*. For example, $(3, 4, 5)$ is a primitive Pythagorean triplet. Although $(30, 40, 50)$ is also a Pythagorean triplet, but it is not primitive.

- ☞ *iii.* If $a + b + c = k$ then by property ☞ *i*, $1 \leq a < k/3$, $a < b$, $c = k - a - b$. These conditions will be used to set the bounds for finding a, b and c.

- ☞ *iv.* We can ignore testing $\gcd(a, b, c) = 1$ since the Problem says "*There exists exactly one Pythagorean triplet for which $a + b + c = 1000$.*"

If we use a naïve algorithm with three loops for finding (a, b, c) as follows,

Algorithm Naïve E9
Input: MN = 1000
Output: (a, b, c) integers,

```
                    a + b + c = MN,
                    a² + b² = c²
    begin
        for a ← 1 to MN do
            for b ← 1 to MN do
                for c ← 1 to MN do
                    if (a + b + c = MN) and (a² + b² = c²)
                        then return a × b × c;
                    endif
                endfor c
            endfor b
        endfor a
    end Naïve E9
```

then the computing time will be about $1000^3 = 1$ billion. The property ℘ *iii* gives a reduced version as follows,

```
Algorithm E9
Input: MN = 1000
Output: (a,b,c) integers,
            a + b + c = MN,
            a² + b² = c²
begin
    for a ← 1 to (MN div 3) do
        for b ← a + 1 to ((MN − a) div 2) do
            c ← MN − a − b;
            if (a² + b² = c²)
                then return a × b × c;
            endif
        endfor b
    endfor a
end E9
```

The computing time of algorithm E9 is about $300 \times 600 = 180000$, which is faster than naïve version 5000 times.

We can improve the computing as follows. Replacing c by $1000-(a+b)$ in the Pythagorean condition, we get

$$a^2 + b^2 = (1000 - (a + b))^2 = 1000000 + a^2 + b^2 + 2(ab - 1000(a + b))$$

After reducing, we get

$$500000 + ab = 1000(a + b) \qquad (9.1)$$

Algorithm E9A is constructed on the equality (9.1).

```
Algorithm E9A
Input: MN = 1000
Output:  (a, b, c) integers,
            a + b + c = MN,
            a² + b² = c²
begin
    for a ← 1 to (MN div 3) do
        for b ← a + 1 to ((MN − a) div 2) do
            if 500000 + a×b = 1000×(a + b)
                then return a×b×(MN − a − b);
            endif
        endfor b
    endfor a
end E9A
```

Furthermore, the equality (9.1) also gives

$$a = 1000(500 - b) / (1000 - b) \qquad (9.2)$$

Setting $m = 1000 - b$, we have $500 - b = m - 500$. Replacing in (9.2) $1000 - b$ by m and $500 - b$ by $m - 500$, we obtain

$$a = 1000(m - 500) / m = (1000m - 500000) / m = 1000 - (500000 / m)$$

Thus, we get

$$a = 1000 - (500000 / m) \qquad (9.3)$$

(9.1) - (9.3) show that $b < 500$, $m > 500$, and $m \mid 500000$, since a is a positive integer. These remarks give the next algorithm E9B with the computing time about 500.

Algorithm E9B
Input: MN = 1000
Output: (a, b, c) integers,
$\quad\quad\quad$ a + b + c = MN,
$\quad\quad\quad$ $a^2 + b^2 = c^2$
begin
$\quad$ // m = MN − b
$\quad$ for m ← 501 to MN do
$\quad\quad$ if (500000 mod m = 0) then
$\quad\quad$ a ← MN − (500000 div m);
$\quad\quad$ b ← MN − m;
$\quad\quad$ c ← MN − a − b;
$\quad\quad$ return (a×b×c);
$\quad\quad$ endif
$\quad$ endfor m
end E9B

C++ Program

```
/************************************************
  Problem 9. Special Pythagorean triplet
  Answer = 31875000,
  Time of E19A = 0.03 sec.
  Time of E19B = 0.02 sec.
************************************************/
#include <iostream>

using namespace std;

int E9A() {
  int a, b, c;
  int maxb;
  int result; // abc
  for (a = 1; a <= 333; ++a) {
    maxb = (1000-a)/ 2;
    for (b = a+1; b <= maxb; ++b) {
      if (500000 + a*b == 1000*(a + b)) {
        c = 1000-(a+b);
        cout << "\n a = " << a << "  b = " << b
          << "  c = " << c;
        result = a*b*c;
        cout << "\n Result = " << result;
```

```
                return (result);
        } // if
      } // for b
   } // for a
} // E9A

int E9B() {
   int a, b, c;
   int result; // abc
   int m = 1000;
   int x = 1000;
   int y = x*500; // 500000
   for (m = 501; m < x; ++m)
     if (y % m == 0) {
         a = x - (y / m);
         b = x - m;
         c =  x - a - b;
         cout << "\n a = " << a << "  b = " << b
              << "  c = " << c;
         result = a*b*c;
         cout << "\n Result = " << result;
         return (result);
     } // if
} // E9B

main() {
   E9A(); // 31875000
   E9B(); // 31875000
   cout << "\n   T H E    E N D . ";
   return 0;
}
```

Free Pascal Program

```
(*********************************************
   Problem 9. Special Pythagorean triplet
   Answer = 31875000,
   Time of E19A = 0.03 sec.
   Time of E19B = 0.02 sec.
*********************************************)

type int =  longint;
```

```
function E9A: int;
  var a, b, c: int;
  maxb: int;
  result: int; // abc
begin
  for a := 1 to 333 do
  begin
    maxb := (1000-a) div 2;
    for b := a+1 to maxb do
      if (500000 + a*b = 1000*(a + b)) then
      begin
        c := 1000 - a - b;
        result := a*b*c;
        writeln(' a = ', a, ' b = ', b, ' c = ', c);
        writeln(' Result = ', result);
        exit(result);
      end; // if
  end; // for a
end; // E9A

function E9B: int;
  var a, b, c: int;
  result: int; // abc
  m, x, y: int;
begin
  x := 1000;
  y := 500*x; // 500000
  // m = 1000 - b
  for m := 501 to 1000 do
    if (y mod m) = 0 then
    begin
      a := x - (y div m);
      b := x - m;
      c := x - a - b;
      result := a*b*c;
      writeln(' a = ', a, ' b = ', b, ' c = ', c);
      writeln(' Result = ', result);
      exit(result);
    end; // if
end; // E9B

BEGIN
  writeln(' E9A: ',E9A); // 31875000
  writeln(' E9B: ',E9B); // 31875000
```

```
   writeln(' T H E    E N D . ');
   readln;
END.
```

Java Program

```
/*******************************************
   Problem 9. Special Pythagorean triplet
   Answer = 31875000,
   Time of E19A = 0.03 sec.
   Time of E19B = 0.02 sec.
*******************************************/

public class E9 {
  E9(){
    E9A();
    E9B();
    } // E9

private int E9A(){
  int a = 0, b = 0, c = 0;
  int maxb = 0;
  int result = 0; // abc
  for (a = 1; a <= 300; ++a) {
    maxb = (1000-a) / 2;
    for (b = a+1; b <= maxb; ++b) {
      if (500000 + a*b == 1000*(a+b)){
        c = 1000 - a - b;
        result = a*b*c;
        System.out.println(" a = " + a + " b = " + b
            + " c = " + c);
        System.out.println(" Result = "+result);
        return result;
      } // if
    } // for b
  } // for a
  return result;
} // E9A

private int E9B(){
  int a = 0, b = 0, c = 0;
  int result = 0; // abc
```

```
int x = 1000;
int y = 500*x; // 500000
int m = 0; // n = 1000 - b
for (m = 501; m < x; ++m)
  if ((y % m) == 0){
    b = x - m;
    a = x - (y / m);
    c = x - a - b;
    result = a*b*c;
    System.out.println(" a = " + a + " b = " + b
        + " c = " + c);
    System.out.println(" Result = "+result);
    return result;
  } // if
  return result;
} // E9B
} // class E9
```

Comment

We can find directly such a divisor m of 500000 that $500 < m < 1000$. Recall that (a, b, c) is a unique triplet. It follows that $m = 1000 - b$ is a unique factor of 500000 and $500 < m < 1000$. Since $500000 = 2^5 \times 5^6$, it follows that $m = 2^u 5^v$ for some $0 \le u \le 5$ and $0 \le v \le 6$. In the other hand, $500000 = 2^3 \times (2 \times 5)^2 \times 5^4 = 800 \times 625$. To find the value of m, we distinguish two cases:

- Case $m = 800$. We have, $b = 1000 - m = 200$; 500000 div $m = 625$; $a = 1000 - 625 = 375 > b = 200$. This contradicts the suggestion that $a < b$.

- Case $m = 625$. We have, $b = 1000 - m = 375$; 500000 div $m = 800$; $a = 1000 - 800 = 200 < b = 375$.

Thus, the case $m = 625$ is accepted and returns $a = 200$, $b = 375$, $c = 425$ and $abc = 31875000$.

Problem 10. Summation of primes

The sum of the primes below 10 is $2 + 3 + 5 + 7 = 17$.

Find the sum of all the primes below two million.

Algorithm

After calling Sieve(2000000) (see Problem 7) we simply take the sum of all primes in the sieve.

```
Algorithm PrimeSum
Input: Integer n > 1
Output: Sum of all primes ≤ n.
begin
    Sieve(n);
    sum ← 0;
    for each prime p in sieve do
        sum ← sum + p;
    endfor
    return sum;
endPrimeSum
```

C++ Program

```
/****************************************
  Problem 10. Summation of primes
  Answer = 142913828922, Time = 0.4 sec.
 ****************************************/
#include <iostream>
#include <math.h>
#include <bitset>

using namespace std;

const int MN = 2000000;
bitset<MN+1> p; // p[0] ... p[2000000]

typedef unsigned long long Long; // 64 bit size

// Sieve of Eratosthenes
```

```
void Sieve(int n) {
  int i, j, n2, sq = (int)sqrt(n);
  p.set(); // all p[i] = 1 (true)
  for (i = 2; i <= sq; ++i)
    if (p[i]) // p[i] = 1, i is a prime
      for (j = i*i; j <= n; j += i)
      p[j] = 0; // delete j
} // Sieve

Long Sum(int n) {
  Long s = 2; // 2 is the first prime
  Sieve(n); // Sieve of Eratosthenes
  // For each odd number
  for (int i = 3; i <= n; i += 2)
    if (p[i]) s += i; // i is prime
  return s;
} //Sum

main() {
  cout << Sum(MN); // 142913828922
  cout << "\n T H E   E N D .";
  return 0;
}
```

Free Pascal Program

In Free Pascal we use a Boolean array b to mark prime or not.

b[i]= true if i is a prime,

b[i]= false if i is not a prime.

```
(*****************************************
  Problem 10. Summation of primes
  Answer = 142913828922, Time = 0.4 sec.
*****************************************)

const MN = 2000000; NL = #13#10;

type int = longint;

var b: array[1..MN] of Boolean;

// Sieve of Eratosthenes: Cac so nguyen to <= n
procedure Sieve(n: int);
```

```
  var i, j: int;
begin
  fillchar(b, sizeof(b), true); // all b[i] true
  for i := 2 to round(sqrt(n)) do
    if b[i] then // b[i] = true, i is a prime
    begin
      j := i*i;
      while j <= n do
      begin
        b[j] := false; // delete j
        inc(j, i); // j := j + i
      end; // while
    end;// if
end; // Sieve

function Sum(n: int): int64;
  var i: int;
  s: int64;
begin
  Sieve(n);
  s := 2;
  i := 3;
  // Scan only odd numbers
  while i <= n do
  begin
    if b[i] then s := s + i; // i is a prime
    inc(i,2);
  end; // while
  exit(s);
end; // Sum

BEGIN
  writeln(Sum(MN)); // 142913828922
  writeln(NL, ' T H E   E N D .');
  readln;
END.
```

Java Program

```
/****************************************
   Problem 10. Summation of primes
   Answer = 142913828922, Time = 0.4 sec.
****************************************/
import java.util.BitSet;
```

```java
public class E10 {
  private int MN = 2000000;
  private BitSet p = new BitSet(MN+1);

  E10() {
    sieve(MN);
    System.out.println(sum(MN));
    // 142913828922
  } // E10

  // All primes <= n
  private void sieve(int n){
    p.clear();
    int sq = (int)Math.sqrt(n);
    boolean prime = false;
    for(int i = 2; i <= sq; ++i) {
    if (p.get(i) == prime) {
      for (int j = i*i; j < n ; j += i)
        p.set(j);
    } // if
    } // for
  }// sieve

  private long sum(int n){
    long s = 2;
    for(int i = 3; i <= n; ++i)
    if (!p.get(i)) s += i;
    return s;
  } // sum
} // class E10
```

Problem 11. Largest product in a grid

In the 20 ×20 grid below, four numbers along a diagonal line have been marked in red.

```
08 02 22 97 38 15 00 40 00 75 04 05 07 78 52 12 50 77 91 08
49 49 99 40 17 81 18 57 60 87 17 40 98 43 69 48 04 56 62 00
81 49 31 73 55 79 14 29 93 71 40 67 53 88 30 03 49 13 36 65
52 70 95 23 04 60 11 42 69 24 68 56 01 32 56 71 37 02 36 91
22 31 16 71 51 67 63 89 41 92 36 54 22 40 40 28 66 33 13 80
24 47 32 60 99 03 45 02 44 75 33 53 78 36 84 20 35 17 12 50
32 98 81 28 64 23 67 10 26 38 40 67 59 54 70 66 18 38 64 70
67 26 20 68 02 62 12 20 95 63 94 39 63 08 40 91 66 49 94 21
24 55 58 05 66 73 99 26 97 17 78 78 96 83 14 88 34 89 63 72
21 36 23 09 75 00 76 44 20 45 35 14 00 61 33 97 34 31 33 95
78 17 53 28 22 75 31 67 15 94 03 80 04 62 16 14 09 53 56 92
16 39 05 42 96 35 31 47 55 58 88 24 00 17 54 24 36 29 85 57
86 56 00 48 35 71 89 07 05 44 44 37 44 60 21 58 51 54 17 58
19 80 81 68 05 94 47 69 28 73 92 13 86 52 17 77 04 89 55 40
04 52 08 83 97 35 99 16 07 97 57 32 16 26 26 79 33 27 98 66
88 36 68 87 57 62 20 72 03 46 33 67 46 55 12 32 63 93 53 69
04 42 16 73 38 25 39 11 24 94 72 18 08 46 29 32 40 62 76 36
20 69 36 41 72 30 23 88 34 62 99 69 82 67 59 85 74 04 36 16
20 73 35 29 78 31 90 01 74 31 49 71 48 86 81 16 23 57 05 54
01 70 54 71 83 51 54 69 16 92 33 48 61 43 52 01 89 19 67 48.
```

The product of these numbers is $26 \times 63 \times 78 \times 14 = 1788696$.

What is the greatest product of four adjacent numbers in any direction (up, down, left, right, or diagonally) in the 20 × 20 grid?

Algorithm

The aim of the problem is training a method of scanning elements in a two-dimensional matrix. Let ss be the given matrix of size 20 × 20 and @ be the cell `ss[i][j]`, $0 \leq i, j \leq 19$. We need to take the products of four adjacent numbers from @ along to the four directions as follows:

```
Right:       ss[i][j]*ss[i][j+1]*ss[i][j+2]*ss[i][j+3];
Down:        ss[i][j]*ss[i+1][j]*ss[i+2][j]*ss[i+3][j];
Right-Down:  ss[i][j]*ss[i+1][j+1]*ss[i+2][j+2]*ss[i+3][j+3];
Left-Down:   ss[i][j]*ss[i+1][j-1]*ss[i+2][j-2]*ss[i+3][j-3].
```

At each step we get the maximum product and save it to a variable pmax.

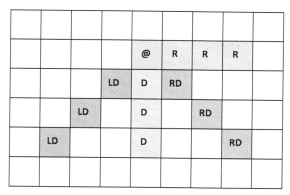

R: Right, D: Down, RD: Right-Down, LD: Left-Down

Of course, we need to control the range of the indexes i and j. For example, if we scan from @ = ss[1][18] then only two directions D and LD will be considered; R and RD will be ignored. Two constants GSIZE = 20 and LIM = 17 are used in programs to maintain the boundaries of i and j.

C++ program

```
/***********************************************
  Problem 11. Largest product in a grid
  Answer = 70600674, Time = 0.1 sec.
***********************************************/
#include <iostream>
#include <math.h>
#include <windows.h>

using namespace std;

const char GSIZE = 20; // grid size
const char LIM = 17;

char ss[GSIZE][GSIZE] = {
{8,2,22,97,38,15,0,40,0,75,4,5,7,78,52,12,50,77,91,8},
{49,49,99,40,17,81,18,57,60,87,17,40,98,43,69,48, 4,56,62,0},
{81,49,31,73,55,79,14,29,93,71,40,67,53,88,30, 3,49,13,36,65},
{52,70,95,23, 4,60,11,42,69,24,68,56, 1,32,56,71,37, 2,36,91},
{22,31,16,71,51,67,63,89,41,92,36,54,22,40,40,28,66,33,13,80},
{24,47,32,60,99, 3,45, 2,44,75,33,53,78,36,84,20,35,17,12,50},
```

```
   {32,98,81,28,64,23,67,10,26,38,40,67,59,54,70,66,18,38,64,70},
   {67,26,20,68, 2,62,12,20,95,63,94,39,63, 8,40,91,66,49,94,21},
   {24,55,58, 5,66,73,99,26,97,17,78,78,96,83,14,88,34,89,63,72},
   {21,36,23, 9,75, 0,76,44,20,45,35,14, 0,61,33,97,34,31,33,95},
   {78,17,53,28,22,75,31,67,15,94, 3,80, 4,62,16,14, 9,53,56,92},
   {16,39, 5,42,96,35,31,47,55,58,88,24, 0,17,54,24,36,29,85,57},
   {86,56, 0,48,35,71,89, 7, 5,44,44,37,44,60,21,58,51,54,17,58},
   {19,80,81,68, 5,94,47,69,28,73,92,13,86,52,17,77, 4,89,55,40},
   {04,52, 8,83,97,35,99,16, 7,97,57,32,16,26,26,79,33,27,98,66},
   {88,36,68,87,57,62,20,72, 3,46,33,67,46,55,12,32,63,93,53,69},
   { 4,42,16,73,38,25,39,11,24,94,72,18, 8,46,29,32,40,62,76,36},
   {20,69,36,41,72,30,23,88,34,62,99,69,82,67,59,85,74,04,36,16},
   {20,73,35,29,78,31,90, 1,74,31,49,71,48,86,81,16,23,57, 5,54},
   {1,70,54,71,83,51,54,69,16,92,33,48,61,43,52, 1,89,19,67,48}};

int pmax;

void Right(int i, int j) {
  int p = ss[i][j]*ss[i][j+1]*ss[i][j+2]*ss[i][j+3];
  if (p > pmax) pmax = p;
} // Right

void Down(int i, int j) {
  int p = ss[i][j]*ss[i+1][j]*ss[i+2][j]*ss[i+3][j];
  if (p > pmax) pmax = p;
} // Down

void RightDown(int i, int j) {
  int p =
ss[i][j]*ss[i+1][j+1]*ss[i+2][j+2]*ss[i+3][j+3];
  if (p > pmax) pmax = p;
} // RightDown

void LeftDown(int i, int j) {
   int p =
   ss[i][j]*ss[i+1][j-1]*ss[i+2][j-2]*ss[i+3][j-3];
  if (p > pmax) pmax = p;
} // LeftDown

void E11() {
  int i, j;
  pmax = 0;
  for (i = 0; i < GSIZE; ++i) {
    for (j = 0; j < GSIZE; ++j) {
      if (j < LIM) Right(i,j);
```

```
      if (i < LIM) Down(i,j);
      if (i < LIM && j < LIM) RightDown(i,j);
      if (i < LIM && j > 2) LeftDown(i,j);
    } // for j
  } // for i
  cout << pmax;
} // E11

main() {
  E11(); // 70600674
  cout << "\n  T H E    E N D .";
  return 0;
}
```

Free Pascal program

```
(*****************************************
  Problem 11. Largest product in a grid
  Answer = 70600674, Time = 0.1 sec.
*****************************************)

const GSIZE = 20; // Grid size
LIM = 18;

const ss: array[1..GSIZE,1..GSIZE] of byte = (
( 8, 2,22,97,38,15, 0,40, 0,75, 4, 5, 7,78,52,12,50,77,91, 8),
(49,49,99,40,17,81,18,57,60,87,17,40,98,43,69,48, 4,56,62, 0),
(81,49,31,73,55,79,14,29,93,71,40,67,53,88,30, 3,49,13,36,65),
(52,70,95,23, 4,60,11,42,69,24,68,56, 1,32,56,71,37, 2,36,91),
(22,31,16,71,51,67,63,89,41,92,36,54,22,40,40,28,66,33,13,80),
(24,47,32,60,99, 3,45, 2,44,75,33,53,78,36,84,20,35,17,12,50),
(32,98,81,28,64,23,67,10,26,38,40,67,59,54,70,66,18,38,64,70),
(67,26,20,68, 2,62,12,20,95,63,94,39,63, 8,40,91,66,49,94,21),
(24,55,58, 5,66,73,99,26,97,17,78,78,96,83,14,88,34,89,63,72),
(21,36,23, 9,75, 0,76,44,20,45,35,14, 0,61,33,97,34,31,33,95),
(78,17,53,28,22,75,31,67,15,94, 3,80, 4,62,16,14, 9,53,56,92),
(16,39, 5,42,96,35,31,47,55,58,88,24, 0,17,54,24,36,29,85,57),
(86,56, 0,48,35,71,89, 7, 5,44,44,37,44,60,21,58,51,54,17,58),
(19,80,81,68, 5,94,47,69,28,73,92,13,86,52,17,77, 4,89,55,40),
(04,52, 8,83,97,35,99,16, 7,97,57,32,16,26,26,79,33,27,98,66),
(88,36,68,87,57,62,20,72, 3,46,33,67,46,55,12,32,63,93,53,69),
( 4,42,16,73,38,25,39,11,24,94,72,18, 8,46,29,32,40,62,76,36),
(20,69,36,41,72,30,23,88,34,62,99,69,82,67,59,85,74,04,36,16),
(20,73,35,29,78,31,90, 1,74,31,49,71,48,86,81,16,23,57, 5,54),
(1,70,54,71,83,51,54,69,16,92,33,48,61,43,52,1,89,19,67,48));
```

```
type int = longint;

var pmax: int;

procedure Right(i, j: int);
  var p: int;
begin
   p := ss[i][j]*ss[i][j+1]*ss[i][j+2]*ss[i][j+3];
   if (p > pmax) then pmax := p;
  end; // Right

procedure Down(i, j: int);
  var p: int;
begin
   p := ss[i][j]*ss[i+1][j]*ss[i+2][j]*ss[i+3][j];
   if (p > pmax) then pmax := p;
end; // Down

procedure RightDown(i, j: int);
  var p: int;
begin
  p := ss[i][j]*ss[i+1][j+1]*ss[i+2][j+2]*ss[i+3][j+3];
  if (p > pmax) then pmax := p;
end; // RightDown

procedure LeftDown(i, j: int);
  var p: int;
begin
  p := ss[i][j]*ss[i+1][j-1]*ss[i+2][j-2]*ss[i+3][j-3];
  if (p > pmax) then pmax := p;
end; // LeftDown

procedure E11;
  var i, j: int;
begin
  pmax := 0;
  for i := 1 to GSIZE do
  begin
    for j := 1 to Gsize do
    begin
        if (j < LIM) then Right(i,j);
        if (i < LIM) then Down(i,j);
        if (i < LIM) and (j < LIM) then RightDown(i,j);
        if (i < LIM) and (j > 3) then LeftDown(i,j);
```

```
      end // forj
    end; // for i
    writeln(pmax);
  end; // E11

BEGIN
    E11; // 70600674
    writeln(#13#10, '  T H E    E N D . ');
    readln;
END.
```

Java program

```
/****************************************
  Problem 11. Largest product in a grid
  Answer = 70600674, Time = 0.1 sec.
****************************************/

public class E11 {
private int ss[][] = {
{ 8, 2,22,97,38,15, 0,40, 0,75, 4, 5, 7,78,52,12,50,77,91, 8},
{49,49,99,40,17,81,18,57,60,87,17,40,98,43,69,48, 4,56,62, 0},
{81,49,31,73,55,79,14,29,93,71,40,67,53,88,30, 0,49,13,36,65},
{52,70,95,23, 4,60,11,42,69,24,68,56, 1,32,56,71,37, 2,36,91},
{22,31,16,71,51,67,63,89,41,92,36,54,22,40,40,28,66,33,13,80},
{24,47,32,60,99, 3,45, 2,44,75,33,53,78,36,84,20,35,17,12,50},
{32,98,81,28,64,23,67,10,26,38,40,67,59,54,70,66,18,38,64,70},
{67,26,20,68, 2,62,12,20,95,63,94,39,63, 8,40,91,66,49,94,21},
{24,55,58, 5,66,73,99,26,97,17,78,78,96,83,14,88,34,89,63,72},
{21,36,23, 9,75, 0,76,44,20,45,35,14, 0,61,33,97,34,31,33,95},
{78,17,53,28,22,75,31,67,15,94, 3,80, 4,62,16,14, 9,53,56,92},
{16,39, 5,42,96,35,31,47,55,58,88,24, 0,17,54,24,36,29,85,57},
{86,56, 0,48,35,71,89, 7, 5,44,44,37,44,60,21,58,51,54,17,58},
{19,80,81,68, 5,94,47,69,28,73,92,13,86,52,17,77, 4,89,55,40},
{ 4,52, 8,83,97,35,99,16, 7,97,57,32,16,26,26,79,33,27,98,66},
{88,36,68,87,57,62,20,72, 3,46,33,67,46,55,12,32,63,93,53,69},
{ 4,42,16,73,38,25,39,11,24,94,72,18, 8,46,29,32,40,62,76,36},
{20,69,36,41,72,30,23,88,34,62,99,69,82,67,59,85,74, 4,36,16},
{20,73,35,29,78,31,90, 1,74,31,49,71,48,86,81,16,23,57, 5,54},
{ 1,70,54,71,83,51,54,69,16,92,33,48,61,43,52, 1,89,19,67,48}};

int GSIZE = 20; // grid size
int LIM = 17;
int pmax = 0;

  E11(){
```

```
  int i, j, p, lim;
  pmax = 0;
  for (i = 0; i < GSIZE; ++i) {
    for (j = 0; j < GSIZE; ++j) {
        if (j < LIM) right(i,j);
        if (i < LIM) down(i,j);
        if (i < LIM && j < LIM) rightDown(i,j);
        if (i < LIM && j > 2) leftDown(i,j);
    } // for j
  } // for i
  System.out.println(pmax);    // 70600674
  } // E11

  private void right(int i, int j) {
   int p = ss[i][j]*ss[i][j+1]*ss[i][j+2]*ss[i][j+3];
   if (p > pmax) pmax = p;
  } // right

  private void down(int i, int j) {
   int p = ss[i][j]*ss[i+1][j]*ss[i+2][j]*ss[i+3][j];
   if (p > pmax) pmax = p;
  } // down

  private void rightDown(int i, int j) {
   int p =
  ss[i][j]*ss[i+1][j+1]*ss[i+2][j+2]*ss[i+3][j+3];
   if (p > pmax) pmax = p;
  } // rightDown

  private void leftDown(int i, int j) {
   int p = ss[i][j]*ss[i+1][j-1]*ss[i+2][j-2]*ss[i+3][j-
  3];
   if (p > pmax) pmax = p;
  } // leftDown
} // class E11
```

Comment

You can split the given matrix into five zones and consider each zone
separately (Fig. 11.1).

C++ version

```cpp
void E11B() {
  int i, j;
pmax = 0;
for (i = 0; i < LIM; ++i) {
  for (j = 0; j < 3; ++j) {
    Right(i,j);
    Down(i,j);
    RightDown(i,j);
  } // j = 0
  for (j = 3; j < LIM; ++j) {
    Right(i,j);
    Down(i,j);
    RightDown(i,j);
    LeftDown(i,j);
  } // j = 3
  for (j = LIM; j < GSIZE; ++j) {
    Down(i,j);
    LeftDown(i,j);
  } // j = LIM
} // i
for (i = 17; i < GSIZE; ++i)
  for (j = 0; j < LIM; ++j)
    Right(i,j);
cout << pmax;
} // E11B
```

Free Pascal version

```pascal
procedure E11B;
  var i, j: int;
begin
  pmax := 0;
  for i := 1 to 17 do
  begin
    for j := 1 to 3 do
    begin
      Right(i,j);
      Down(i,j);
      RightDown(i,j);
    end; // j = 1
    for j := 4 to 17 do
    begin
```

```
      Right(i,j);
      Down(i,j);
      RightDown(i,j);
      LeftDown(i,j);
    end; // j = 4
      for j := 18 to 20 do
      begin
        Down(i,j);
        LeftDown(i,j);
      end; // j = 18
  end; // i
  for i := 18 to 20 do
    for j := 1 to 17 do
      Right(i,j);
  writeln(pmax);
end; // E11B
```

Java version

```java
private void E11B() {
  int i, j;
  pmax = 0;
  for (i = 0; i < LIM; ++i) {
    for (j = 0; j < 3; ++j) {
      right(i,j);
      down(i,j);
      rightDown(i,j);
    } // j = 0
    for (j = 3; j < LIM; ++j) {
      right(i,j);
      down(i,j);
      rightDown(i,j);
      leftDown(i,j);
    } // j = 3
    for (j = LIM; j < GSIZE; ++j) {
      down(i,j);
      leftDown(i,j);
    } // j = LIM
  } // i
  for (i = 17; i < GSIZE; ++i)
    for (j = 0; j < LIM; ++j)
      right(i,j);
  System.out.println(pmax);   // 70600674
} // E11B
```

Problem 12. Highly divisible triangular number

The sequence of triangle numbers is generated by adding the natural numbers. So the 7th triangle number would be $1 + 2 + 3 + 4 + 5 + 6 + 7 = 28$. The first ten terms would be:

1, 3, 6, 10, 15, 21, 28, 36, 45, 55, ...

Let us list the factors of the first seven triangle numbers:

  1: 1
  3: 1, 3
  6: 1, 2, 3, 6
  10: 1, 2, 5, 10
  15: 1, 3, 5, 15
  21: 1, 3, 7, 21
  28: 1, 2, 4, 7, 14, 28

We can see that 28 is the first triangle number to have over five divisors.

What is the value of the first triangle number to have over five hundred divisors?

Understanding

Let us write the first ten triangle numbers with their factors:

N		Triangle Number	Factors	Number of factors
1	1	1	1	1
2	1 + 2	3	1, 3	2
3	1 + 2 + 3	6	1, 2, 3, 6	4
4	1 + 2 + 3 + 4	10	1, 2, 5, 10	4
5	1 + 2 + 3 + 4 + 5	15	1, 3, 5, 15	4
6	1 + 2 + 3 + 4 + 5 + 6	21	1, 3, 7, 21	4
7	1 + 2 + 3 + 4 + 5 + 6 + 7	28	1, 2, 4, 7, 14, 28	6
8	1 + 2 + 3 + 4 + 5 + 6 + 7 + 8	36	1, 2, 3, 4, 6, 9, 12, 18, 36	9
9	1 + 2 + 3 + 4 + 5 + 6 + 7 + 8 + 9	45	1, 3, 5, 9, 15, 45	6
10	1 + 2 + 3 + 4 + 5 + 6 + 7 + 8 + 9 + 10	55	1, 5, 11, 55	4

We see that the 7th triangle number has six factors 1, 2, 4, 7, 14 and 28.

Algorithm

Let $\tau(n)$ be a function giving the number of factors of a natural number n. A simple method of computing function $\tau(n)$ is based on the divisibility as follows. If a is a factor of n, namely, $n = ab$, then b also is another factor of n if $b \neq a$. So, all factors of a given natural number n can be written as symmetrical pairwises (a, b) where $a \neq b$ and $ab = n$ (*Fig.* 12.1).

Fig 12.1 *The set of factors of 28.*   *The set of factors of 36.*
$\tau(28) = 6$ $\tau(36) = 9$

We consider the case, when n is a *perfect square*, that it is a product of some integer with itself, $n = a^2 = a \times a$. For example, 36 is a perfect square number, since it can be written as 6×6.

For each pair (a, b), $ab = n$, if $a \neq b$ then the value of $\tau(n)$ is increased by 2, otherwise, if $a = b$, namely, when n is a perfect square, then the value of $\tau(n)$ is increased by 1. Since $1n = n$ and $ab = n$, we need only scan for each a from 2 to $\lfloor \sqrt{n} \rfloor$.

```
Algorithm Tau
Input: integer n > 0.
Output: τ(n): number of factors of n.
begin
    s ← ⌊√n⌋;
    count ← 2; // n has two special divisors 1 and n
    for d ← 2 to s do
        if (n mod d = 0) then count ← count + 2 endif
    endfor
    if (s × s = n) then return (count – 1)
        else return count;
    endif
endTau
```

Denoting by $T(n)$ the nth triangle number, we see

$T(1) = 1$,

$T(n) = T(n-1) + n; \ n > 1$.

The first version E12A for the problem is very simple as follows.

Algorithm E12A
Input: integer constant V = 500.
Output: The first triangle number tn: τ(tn) > V.
begin
tn ← 0; n ← 0;
repeat
n ← n +1; // the next n
tn ← tn + n; // the next triangle number tn
until Tau(tn) > v;
return tn;
endE12A

C++ program

```
/****************************************************
    Problem 12. Highly divisible triangular number
    Version E12A.
    Answer = 76576500, Time = 0.4 sec.
****************************************************/
#include <iostream>
#include <math.h>

using namespace std;

const int V = 500;

// Number of divisors of n
int Tau(int n) {
    int s = 2; // if n > 1 then n has two
            // trivial factors 1 and n
    int sqr = int(sqrt(n));
    for (int d = 2; d <= sqr; ++d)
```

```cpp
      if (n % d == 0) s += 2;
    return (sqr*sqr == n) ? s - 1 : s;
} // Tau

void E12A() {
    int tn = 0; // Triangle Number;
    int n = 0;
    do {
      ++n;
      tn += n;
    } while (Tau(tn) <= V);
    cout << "\n Result of E12A: " << tn;
} // E12A

main() {
    E12A(); // 76576500
    cout << "\n  T H E    E N D .";
    return 0;
}
```

Free Pascal Program

```pascal
(* * * * * * * * * * * * * * * * * * * * * * * * * * * * * * * * * * * * * * * * *
   Problem 12. Highly divisible triangular number
   Version E12A.
   Answer = 76576500, Time = 0.4 sec.
* * * * * * * * * * * * * * * * * * * * * * * * * * * * * * * * * * * * * * * *)

type int = longint;

const V = 500;

// Number of divisors of n
function Tau(n: int): int;
 var s, sqr, d: int;
 begin
   s := 2; // if n > 1 then n has two
           // trivial factors 1 and n
   sqr := round(sqrt(n));
   for d := 2 to sqr do
     if (n mod d = 0) then inc(s,2);
   if (sqr*sqr = n) then exit(s - 1) else exit(s);
 end; // Tau
```

```
procedure E12A;
  var n, tn: int;
  begin
    n := 0; tn := 0;
    repeat
      inc(n); inc(tn,n);
    until Tau(tn) > V;
    writeln(' Result of E12B: ', tn);
end; // E12A

BEGIN
  E12A; // 76576500
  writeln(' T H E   E N D .');
  readln;
END.
```

Java Program

```
/*****************************************************
  Problem 12. Highly divisible triangular number
  Version E12A.
  Answer = 76576500, Time = 0.4 sec.
*****************************************************/
public class E12 {
private int V = 500;

E12(){
    E12A();
} // E12

private void E12A() {
    int n = 0, tn = 0;
    do  {
        ++n; tn += n;
    } while (Tau(tn) <= V);
    System.out.println("\n Result of E12B: " + tn);
  } // E12A

// Number of divisors of n
  private int Tau(int n) {
      int s = 2; // if n > 1 then n has two
                 // trivial divisors 1 and n
      int sqr = (int)Math.sqrt(n);
```

```
    for (int d = 2; d <= sqr; ++d) {
        if (n % d == 0) s += 2;
    } // for
    return (sqr*sqr == n) ? s-1 : s;
  } // Tau
} // class E12
```

Enhancement

Since function $\tau(x)$ is complicated then we will try to increase its computability. Our goal is focusing to the computability of $\tau(n)$ and $\tau(T(n))$.

We know that

$$T(n) = 1 + 2 + \cdots + n = \frac{n(n+1)}{2} \qquad (Gauss)$$

If n is even, $n = 2k$, then $T(n) = 2k(2k+1)/2 = k(2k+1) = k(n+1)$

If n is odd, $n = 2k+1$, then $T(n) = (2k+1)(2k+2)/2 = (k+1)(2k+1) = (k+1)n$.

First, we prove that k and $2k+1$ are *relatively primes*, that they have greatest common divisor $(k, 2k+1) = 1$. Indeed, using properties gcd6 and gcd8 of Problem 5, we get

$$(k, 2k+1) = (k, (2k+1) \bmod k) = (k, 1) = 1$$

Likewise, $k+1$ and $2k+1$ are relatively primes too. It is because

$(k+1, 2k+1) = (k+1, ((k+1)+k) \bmod (k+1)) = (k+1, k) = ((k+1) \bmod k, k)$
$= (1, k) = 1$.

Following elementary number theory, we know that $\tau(n)$ is a *multiplicative function*, that if a and b are relatively primes, $(a, b) = 1$, then $\tau(ab) = \tau(a)\tau(b)$. We have,

If n is an even number, $n = 2k$, then $T(n) = k(2k+1)$, so $\tau(T(n)) = \tau(k)\tau(2k+1)$, since k and $2k + 1$ are relatively primes.

If n is an odd number, $n = 2k+1$, then $T(n) = (k+1)(2k+1)$, so $\tau(T(n)) = \tau(k+1)\tau(2k+1)$, since $k+1$ and $n = 2k+1$ are relatively primes.

$$\tau(T(n)) = \begin{cases} \tau(k)\tau(2k+1) = \tau(k)\tau(n+1), & if \ n = 2k \\ \tau(k+1)\tau(2k+1) = \tau(k+1)\tau(n), & if \ n = 2k+1 \end{cases}$$

These equalities give the first draft of algorithm E12B as follows

```
Algorithm E12B
Input: integer constant V = 500.
Output: The first triangle number tn: τ(tn) > V.
begin
    k ← 0; n ← 1;
    while true do
        k ← k+1;
        n ← n + 1; // n = 2k is even
        a ← n; // a = 2k
        ta ← Tau(k)×Tau(a+1); // degree(2,n)
        if (ta > V) then
            return n×(n+1) div 2; // T(n)
        endif
        n ← n + 1; // n = 2k+1 is odd
        b ← n; // b = 2k+1
        tb ← Tau(k+1)×Tau(b);
        if (tb > V) then
            return n×(n+1) div 2; // T(n)
        endif
    endwhile
EndE12B.
```

We see that for each value k we compute two values of Tau(n) for even case, $n = 2k$ and for odd case, $n = 2k+1$. Therefore, we need to call function Tau for four times, namely, Tau(k), Tau($a+1$), Tau($k+1$) and Tau(b), where $a = 2k$, $b = 2k+1$. Since $a+1 = b = 2k+1$, we need compute Tau only for one of them. If the value of a is an odd number, $a = 3, 5, 7, \ldots$ then we can reuse Tau(b) for setting Tau(a), since all the values of b are only odd numbers and Tau(b) is computed before a. So, we need only compute Tau(a) with even values of a.

Again, following the fundamental theorem of arithmetic, we know that if n is represented in the form of prime factorization as in Problem 3,

$$n = p_1^{m_1} p_2^{m_2} \ldots p_k^{m_k}$$

where $k > 0$, $p_1 < p_2 < \ldots < p_k$ are primes, $m_i \geq 1$ and m_i is called the *degree* of prime factor p_i in n, $1 \leq i \leq k$,

then

$$\tau(n) = \prod_{i=1}^{k}(m_i + 1) = \prod_{i=1}^{k}(deg(p_i, n) + 1) \qquad (12.1)$$

where Π is the product symbol, $deg(p_i, n) = m_i$ is the degree of prime p_i in n.

For example, with $n = 28 = 2^2 \times 7$, we have, $deg(2, 28) = 2$, $deg(7, 28) = 1$, and for all primes $p \notin \{2, 7\}$, $deg(p, 28) = 0$. So, $deg(p, n)$, p prime, is the *maximum number* k such that $p^k \mid n$. Using formula (12.1) we have $\tau(28) = (2+1)(1+1) = 3 \times 2 = 6$.

Now we try to use formula (12.1) to get a method for computing $\tau(a)$ with even values of a, $a = 2u$.

Let $a = 2u > 0$, $deg(2, u) = d$. Then $u = m2^d$ for some odd integer m. That $a = 2u = 2(m2^d) = m2^{d+1}$, hence $deg(2, a) = d+1 = deg(2, u)+1$. Since m is odd, 2^{d+1} is even, and $2^d = 1$ if $d = 0$ and 2^d is even if $d > 0$, this implies $(m, 2^d) = 1$ and $(m, 2^{d+1}) = 1$. Applying property of multiplicative function τ and expression (12.1) we get

$$\tau(u) = \tau(m2^d) = \tau(m)\tau(2^d) = \tau(m)(\deg(2, u)+1) \tag{12.2}$$

$$\tau(a) = \tau(m2^{d+1}) = \tau(m)\tau(2^{d+1}) = \tau(m)(\deg(2, a)+1) \tag{12.3}$$

$$\deg(2, a) = d + 1 = \deg(2, u) + 1 \tag{12.4}$$

(12.2) gives

$$\tau(m) = \frac{\tau(u)}{\deg(2, u) + 1} \tag{12.5}$$

Replacing $\tau(m)$ of (12.5) in (12.3) we get

$$\tau(a) = \frac{\tau(u)}{\deg(2, u) + 1}(\deg(2, a) + 1)$$

Using (12.4) we get

$$\tau(a) = \frac{\tau(u)}{\deg(2, a)}(\deg(2, a) + 1) \tag{12.6}$$
$$= \tau(u) + (\tau(u) \text{ div } \deg(2, \text{a}))$$

Expressions (12.4) and (12.6) show that if we know $\tau(u)$ and $deg(2, u)$ then we can compute $\tau(a)$ and $deg(2, a)$.

Using an array t[] to save the values of $\tau(x)$ and an array d[] to save the values of *degree* of 2 in x we can construct an enhancement version of algorithm E12A, named E12B.

```
Algorithm E12B
Input: integer constant V = 500.
Output: The first triangle number tn: τ(tn) > V.
begin
    k ← 0; n ← 1;
    while true do
        k ← k+1;
        n ← n + 1; // n = 2k is even
        d[n] ← d[k] + 1; // degree(2,n)
        t[n] ← t[k] + (t[k] div d[n]); // Tau(2k)
        n ← n + 1; // n = 2k+1 is odd
        t[n] ← Tau(n);
        if (t[k]*t[n] > V) then
            tn ← ((n-1)*n) div 2;
```

```
            return tn;
         endif
         if (t[k+1]*t[n] > V) then
            tn ← (n*(n+1)) div 2;
            return tn;
         endif;
      endwhile
   EndE12B.
```

Note that algorithm E12B calls function $\tau(n)$ only one time when n is an odd positive integer.

C++ Program

```
/ * * * * * * * * * * * * * * * * * * * * * * * * * * * * * * * * * * * * * * * * * * * * * * * * * *
   Problem 12. Highly divisible triangular number
   Version E12B.
   Answer = 76576500, Time = 0.03 sec.
 * * * * * * * * * * * * * * * * * * * * * * * * * * * * * * * * * * * * * * * * * * * * * * * * * * /
#include <iostream>
#include <math.h>
#include <windows.h>

using namespace std;

const int V = 500;

const int MN = 12400; // max n = 12375

int t[MN];
int d[MN]; // degree(2,n)

// Number of divisors of n
int Tau(int n) {
  int s = 2; // if n > 1 then n has two
             // trivial factors 1 and n
  int sqr = int(sqrt(n));
  for (int d = 2; d <= sqr; ++d)
    if (n % d == 0) s += 2;
  return (sqr*sqr == n) ? s - 1 : s;
} // Tau

// Tau(T(2k)) = Tau(k)Tau(2k+1)
```

```
// Tau(T(2k+1)) = Tau(k+1)Tau(2k+1)
// Tau(2k) = t[k] + (t[k] div d[n])
void E12B() {
  int k, n;
  memset(t, 0, sizeof(t));
  memset(d, 0, sizeof(d));
  n = 1; t[n] = 1;
  for (k = 1; true; ++k) {
    ++n; // n = 2k
    d[n] = d[k] + 1;
    t[n] = t[k] + (t[k] / d[n]); // Tau(n);
    ++n; // n = 2k+1
    t[n] = Tau(n);
    if (t[k]*t[n] > V) { --n; break; }
    if (t[k+1]*t[n] > V) break;
  } // for
  cout << "\n Result of E12B: " << n*(n+1)/2;
} // E12B

main() {
  E12B(); // 76576500
  cout << "\n  T H E   E N D .";
  return 0;
}
```

Free Pascal program

```
(****************************************************
  Problem 12. Highly divisible triangular number
  Version E12B.
  Answer = 76576500, Time = 0.03 sec.
****************************************************)

type int = longint;

const V = 500;
      MN = 12400; // max n = 12375

var t, d: array[1..MN] of int;

// Number of divisors of n
function Tau(n: int): int;
  var s, sqr, d: int;
```

```
begin
   s := 2; // if n > 1 then n has two
       // trivial factors 1 and n
    sqr := round(sqrt(n));
    for d := 2 to sqr do
     if (n mod d = 0) then inc(s,2);
    if (sqr*sqr = n) then exit(s - 1) else exit(s);
  end; // Tau

// Tau(T(2k)) = Tau(k)Tau(2k+1)
// Tau(T(2k+1)) = Tau(k+1)Tau(2k+1)
// Tau(2k) = t[k] + (t[k] div d[n])
procedure E12B;
  var k, n: int;
begin
  fillchar(t, sizeof(t), 0);
  fillchar(d, sizeof(d), 0);
  n := 1; t[n] := 1;
  k := 0;
  while true do
  begin
    inc(k);
    inc(n); // n = 2k
    d[n] := d[k] + 1;
    t[n] := t[k] + (t[k] div d[n]); // Tau(n);
    inc(n); // n = 2k+1
    t[n] := Tau(n);
    if (t[k]*t[n] > V) then
    begin
      dec(n); break;
    end;
    if (t[k+1]*t[n] > V) then  break;
  end; // while
  writeln(' Result of E12B: ', n*(n+1) div 2);
end; // E12B

BEGIN
  E12B; // 76576500
  writeln(' T H E   E N D .');
  readln;
END.
```

Java Program

```
/*****************************************************
  Problem 12. Highly divisible triangular number
  Version E12B.
  Answer = 76576500, Time = 0.022 sec.
*****************************************************/
public class E12 {
private int V = 500;
private int MAXN = 12400; // max n = 12375
private int [] t = new int[MAXN]; //t[i] = Tau(i)

E12(){
    E12B();
} // E12

// Tau(T(2k)) = Tau(k)Tau(2k+1)
// Tau(T(2k+1)) = Tau(k+1)Tau(2k+1)
// Tau(2k) = t[k] + (t[k] div d[n])
private void E12B() {
  int n = 1, k; // n = 2
  t[n] = 1;
  for (k = 1; true; ++k){
     ++n; t[n] = Tau(n);
     ++n; t[n] = Tau(n);
     if (t[k]*t[n] > V) { --n; break; };
     if (t[k+1]*t[n] > V) break;
  } // for
  System.out.println("\n Result of E12B: " +
                     (n*(n+1)/2));
 } // E12B

 // Number of divisors of n
 int Tau(int n) {
   int s = 2; // if n > 1 then n has two
   // trivial divisors 1 and n
   int sqr = (int)Math.sqrt(n);
   for (int d = 2; d <= sqr; ++d) {
     if (n % d == 0) s += 2;
   } // for
   return (sqr*sqr == n) ? s-1 : s;
 } // Tau
} // class E12
```

Problem 13. Large sum

Work out the first ten digits of the sum of the following one-hundred 50-digit numbers.

```
37107287533902102798797998220837590246510135740250
46376937677490009712648124896970078050417018260538
74324986199524741059474233309513058123726617309629
91942213363574161572522430563301811072406154908250
23067588207539346171171980310421047513778063246676
89261670696623633820136378418383684178734361726757
28112879812849979408065481931592621691275889832738
44274228917432520321923589422876796487670272189318
47451445736001306439091167216856844588711603153276
70386486105843025439939619828917593665686757934951
62176457141856560629502157223196586755079324193331
64906352462741904929101432445813822663347944758178
92575867718337217661963751590579239728245599838407
58203565325359399008402633568948830189458628227828
80181199384826282014278194139940567587151170094390
35398664372827112653829987240784473053190104293586
86515506006295864861532075273371959191420517255829
71693888707715466499115593487603532921714970056938
54370070576826684624621495650076471787294438377604
53282654108756828443191190634694037855217779295145
36123272525000296071075082563815656710885258350721
45876576172410976447339110607218265236877223636045
17423706905851860660448207621209813287860733969412
81142660418086830619328460811191061556940512689692
51934325451728388641918047049293215058642563049483
62467221648435076201727918039944693004732956340691
15732444386908125794514089057706229429197107928209
55037687525678773091862540744969844508330393682126
18336384825330154686196124348767681297534375946515
80386287592878490201521685554828717201219257766954
78182833757993103614740356856449095527097864797581
16726320100436897842553533920931837441497806860984
48403098129077791799088218795327364475675590848030
87086987551392711854517078544161852424320693150332
59959406895756536782107074926966537676326235447210
69793950679652694742597709739166693763042633987085
41052684708299085211399427365734116182760315001271
65378607361501080857009149939512557028198746004375
35829035317434717326932123578154982629742552737307
```

```
9495375976510530594696606768315657437716740187 5275
8890280257173322961917666871381993181104877019 0271
2526768027607800301367868099252546340106163286 6526
3627021854049770558562994658063623799314074625 5962
2407448690823117497779236546625724692332281091 7141
9143028819710328859780666976089293863828502533 3403
3441306557801612781592181500556186883646842009 0470
2305308117281643048762379196984248725503663878 4583
1148769693215490281042402013833512446218144177 3470
6378329949063625966649858761822122522551248676 4533
6772018697169854431241957240991395900895231005 8822
9554825530026352078153229679624948164195386821 8774
7608532713228572311042480345612486769706450799 5236
3777424253541129168427686553892620502491032657 2967
2370191327572567528565324825826546309220705859 6522
2979886027225833191312637514734199488953476574 5501
1849570145487928898485682772607771372140379887 9715
3829820378303147352772158034814451349137322665 1381
3482954382919991818027891652243102739225112286 9539
4095795306640523263253804410005965493915987959 3635
2974615218550237130764225512118369380358038858 4903
4169811622207297718615823667842468915799353296 1922
6246795719440126904387710727504810239089552359 7457
2318970677254791506150550495392297953090112996 7519
8618808822587531452958409925120382900940777077 5672
1130673970830472448381653387350234084564705807 7308
8295917476714036319800818712901187549131054712 6581
9762333104481838626951545633492636657289756340 0500
4284628018351707052783183942588214552122725125 0327
5512160354698120058176216521282765275169129689 7789
3223819573432933994643750190783694576588335239 9886
7550616496518477518073816883786109152735792970 1337
6217784275219262340194239963916804498399317331 2731
3292418570714734956691667468763466091503591467 7504
9951867143023521962889489010242332511691361962 6622
7326746080059154747183079839286853520694694454 0724
7684182252467441716151403642798227334805555621 4818
9714261791034259864720451689398942217982608807 6852
8778364618279934631376775430780936333301898264 2090
1084880252167467088321512018588354322381287695 2786
7132961247478246453863699300904931036361976387 8039
6218407357239979422340623539380833965132740801 1116
6662789198148808779794187687614423003098449085 1411
6066182629368283676474477923918033511098906979 0714
```

```
85786944089552990653640447425576083659976645795096
66024396409905389607120198219976047599490197230297
64913982680032973156037120041377903785566085089252
16730939319872750275468906903707539413042652315011
94809377245048795150954100921645863754710598436791
78639167021187492431995700641917969777599028300699
15368713711936614952811305876380278410754449733078
40789923115535562561142322423255033685442488917353
44889911501440648020369068063960672322193204149535
41503128880339536053299340368006977710650566631954
81234880673210146739058568557934581403627822703280
82616570773948327592232845941706525094512325230608
22918802058777319719839450180888072429661980811197
77158542502016545090413245809786882778948721859617
72107838435069186155435662884062257473692284509516
20849603980134001723930671666823555245252804609722
53503534226472524250874054075591789781264330331690
```

Understanding

Following positional number system, the term *"… the first ten digits"*
can be understood as *"… ten leftmost digits"* or *"… ten rightmost digits"*.
For example, the *first three digits* of number <u>123</u>45<u>678</u> may be 123 if
we take digits by reading or 678 if we take digits by positions. So, we
will give the answer for the both variants.

Positions	7	6	5	4	3	2	1	0
Digits	**1**	**2**	**3**	4	5	**6**	**7**	**8**

Algorithm

The problem requires adding 100 big integers (with 50 digits for each).
If all 100 input numbers are maximum, that they are $c = 9…9$, then the
maximum sum will be

$$100 \times c = 100 \times 9…9 = 9…900$$

and the *length* (number of digits) will be 52.

Suppose the input is given in an array s of 100 strings with length 50. We use an array x with 52 numbers to save the sum. For each line i in s we add number $s[i]$ to x.

```
for i ← 1 to 100 do Add(x, s[i]);
```

Recall that $x[j]$ is a numeric digit, while $s[i][j]$ is a character digit, $1 \le i \le 100$, $1 \le j \le 50$.

It is easy to convert a character digit c to number d.

```
d = c - '0'; // C++ and Java
d = ord(c) - ord('0'); // Free Pascal
```

First, we add digits by columns without carrying, then we propagate carries from right to the left to get the final sum. It follows that the index can be down to the negative value. So, we will set the size of array x to the 52 elements. The following example ilustrates how can get the sum of five 6-digits integer (Fig. 13.1).

$$534974 + 657826 + 246997 + 446299 + 319738$$

Positions		6	5	4	3	2	1	0
Array indexes			0	1	2	3	4	5
			5	3	4	9	7	4
			6	5	7	8	2	6
	+		2	4	6	9	9	7
			4	4	6	2	9	9
			3	1	9	7	3	8
Sums by columns (A)			20	17	32	35	30	34
carry (C = (A+C) div 10)		2	2	3	3	3	3	0
A+C			22	20	35	38	33	34
Final sum (x[i] = (A+C) mod 10)		**2**	**2**	**0**	**5**	**8**	**3**	**4**

Fig.13.1 Adding by columns and propagating carries

C++ Program

```
/********************************************************
  Problem 13. Large sum
  5537376230390876637302048746832985971773659831892672
  Answers:
```

```
   The First ten digits of the sum: 5537376230
   The Last ten digits of the sum: 9831892672
   Time = 0.02 sec.
**********************************************************/

#include <iostream>
#include <math.h>
#include <windows.h>

using namespace std;

const char MN = 52; // max len of the sum
const char LEN = 50; // len of each input number
const int NUM = 100; // number of rows

short x[MN];
short len;

string s[100] = {
"37107287533902102798797998220837590246510135740250",
"46376937677490009712648124896970078050417018260538",
"74324986199524741059474233309513058123726617309629",
"91942213363574161572522430563301811072406154908250",
"23067588207539346171171980310421047513778063246676",
"89261670696623363382013637841838368417873436172675",
"28112879812849979408065481931592621691275889832738",
"44274228917432520321923589422876794687670272189318",
"47451445736001306439091167216856844588711603153276",
"70386486105843025439939619828917593665686757934951",
"62176457141856560629502157223196586755079324193331",
"64906352462741904929101432445813822663347944758178",
"92575867718337217661963751590579239728245598838407",
"58203565325359399008402633568948830189458628227828",
"80181199384826282014278194139940567587151170094390",
"35398664372827112653829987240784473053190104293586",
"86515506006295864861532075273371959191420517255829",
"71693888707715466499115593487603532921714970056938",
"54370070576826684624621495650076471787294438377604",
"53282654108756828443191190634694037855217779295145",
"36123272525000296071075082563815656710885258350721",
"45876576172410976447339110607218265236877223636045",
"17423706905851860660448207621209813287860733969412",
"81142660418086830619328460811191061556940512689692",
"51934325451728388641918047049293215058642563049483",
```

```
"62467221648435076201727918039944693004732956340691",
"15732444386908125794514089057706229429197107928209",
"55037687525678773091862540744969844508330393682126",
"18336384825330154686196124348767681297534375946515",
"80386287592878490201521685554828717201219257766954",
"78182833757993103614740356856449095527097864797581",
"16726320100436897842553539920931837441497806860984",
"48403098129077791799088218795327364475675590848030",
"87086987551392711854517078544161852424320693150332",
"59959406895756536782107074926966537676326235447210",
"69793950679652694742597709739166693763042633987085",
"41052684708299085211399427365734116182760315001271",
"65378607361501080857009149939512557028198746004375",
"35829035317434717326932123578154982629742552737307",
"94953759765105305946966067683156574377167401875275",
"88902802571733229619176668713819931811048770190271",
"25267680276078003013678680992525463401061632866526",
"36270218540497705585629946580636237993140746255962",
"24074486908231174977792365466257246923322810917141",
"91430288197103288597806669760892938638285025333403",
"34413065578016127815921815005561868836468420090470",
"23053081172816430487623791969842487255036638784583",
"11487696932154902810424020138335124462181441773470",
"63783299490636259666498587618221225225512486764533",
"67720186971698544312419572409913959008952310058822",
"95548255300263520781532296796249481641953868218774",
"76085327132285723110424803456124867697064507995236",
"37774242535411291684276865538926205024910326572967",
"23701913275725675285653248258265463092207058596522",
"29798860272258331913126375147341994889534765745501",
"18495701454879288984856827726077713721403798879715",
"38298203783031473527721580348144513491373226651381",
"34829543829199918180278916522431027392251122869539",
"40957953066405232632538044100059654939159879593635",
"29746152185502371307642255121183693803580388584903",
"41698116222072977186158236678424689157993532961922",
"62467957194401269043877107275048102390895523597457",
"23189706772547915061505504953922979530901129967519",
"86188088225875314529584099251203829009407770775672",
"11306739708304724483816533873502340845647058077308",
"82959174767140363198008187129011875491310547126581",
"97623331044818386269515456334926366572897563400500",
"42846280183517070527831839425882145521227251250327",
"55121603546981200581762165212827652751691296897789",
```

```
"32238195734329339946437501907836945765883352399886",
"75506164965184775180738168837861091527357929701337",
"62177842752192623401942399639168044983993173312731",
"32924185707147349566916674687634660915035914677504",
"99518671430235219628894890102423325116913619626622",
"73267460800591547471830798392868535206946944540724",
"76841822524674417161514036427982273348055556214818",
"97142617910342598647204516893989422179826088076852",
"87783646182799346313767754307809363333018982642090",
"10848802521674670883215120185883543223812876952786",
"71329612474782464538636993009049310363619763878039",
"62184073572399794223406235938083396513274080111116",
"66627891981488087797941876876144230030984490851411",
"60661826293682836764744779239180335110989069790714",
"85786944089552990653640447425576083659976645795096",
"66024396409905389607120198219976047599490197230297",
"64913982680032973156037120041377903785566085089252",
"16730939319872750275468906903707539413042652315011",
"94809377245048795150954100921645863754710598436791",
"78639167021187492431995700641917969777599028300699",
"15368713711936614952811305876380278410754449733078",
"40789923115535562561142324232550336854422488917353",
"44889911501440648020369068063960672322193204149535",
"41503128880339536053299340368006977710650566631954",
"81234880673210146739058568557934581403627822703280",
"82616570773948327592232845941706525094512325230608",
"22918802058777319719839450180888072429661980811197",
"77158542502016545090413245809786882778948721859617",
"72107838435069186155435662884062257473692284509516",
"20849603980134001723930671666823555245252804609722",
"53503534226472524250874054075591789781264330331690"
};

// returns the first (leftmost) index of x.
int Carrying() {
  short c, i, j, z;
  c = 0;
  len = LEN+1;
  for (i = LEN-1, j = len; i >= 0; --i, --j) {
    z = x[i]+c;
    x[j] = z % 10;
    c = z / 10;
  } // for
  while (c > 0) {
```

```
    x[j--] = c % 10;
    c /= 10;
    } // while
  return j+1;
} // Carrying

void E13() {
  short col, row, start, j;
  // Take sums by columns
  // Get the first row s[0]
  row = 0;
  for (col = 0; col < LEN; ++col)
    x[col] = s[row][col]-'0';
  // Sum of 100 input lines without carrying
  for (row = 1; row < NUM; ++row)
    for (col = 0; col < LEN; ++col)
      x[col] += (s[row][col]-'0');
  start = Carrying();
  cout << "\n Len = " << len;
  // Print x
  cout << "\n Sum: ";
  for (col = start; col <= len; ++col)
    cout << x[col];
  // Print 10 digits
  cout << "\n The First ten digits of the sum: ";
  j = start+10;
  for (col = start; col < j; ++col)
    cout << x[col];
  start = len-9;
  cout << "\n The  Last ten digits of the sum: ";
  for (col = start; col <= len; ++col)
    cout << x[col];
} // E13

main() {
   E13();
   cout << "\n  T H E   E N D .";
   return 0;
}
```

Free Pascal Program

In Pascal you can declare an array variable and set the beginning values
to it in the section const.

```
(*********************************************************
    Problem 13. Large sum
    5537376230390876637302048746832985971773659831892672
    Answers:
    The First ten digits of the sum: 5537376230
    The Last ten digits of the sum: 9831892672
    Time = 0.02 sec.
*********************************************************)
type int = integer;
const MN = 52;   SLEN = 50;
NUM = 100;  NL = #13#10;
s: array[1..NUM] of string[50] = (
'37107287533902102798797998220837590246510135740250',
'46376937677490009712648124896970078050417018260538',
'74324986199524741059474233309513058123726617309629',
'91942213363574161572522430563301811072406154908250',
'23067588207539346171171980310421047513778063246676',
'89261670696623633820136378418383684178734361726757',
'28112879812849979408065481931592621691275889832738',
'44274228917432520321923589422876796487670272189318',
'47451445736001306439091167216856844588711603153276',
'70386486105843025439939619828917593665686757934951',
'62176457141856560629502157223196586755079324193331',
'64906352462741904929101432445813822663347944758178',
'92575867718337217661963751590579239728245598838407',
'58203565325359399008402633568948830189458628227828',
'80181199384826282014278194139940567587151170094390',
'35398664372827112653829987240784473053190104293586',
'86515506006295864861532075273371959191420517255829',
'71693888707715466499115593487603532921714970056938',
'54370070576826684624621495650076471787294438377604',
'53282654108756828443191190634694037855217779295145',
'36123272525000296071075082563815656710885258350721',
'45876576172410976447339110607218265236877223636045',
'17423706905851860660448207621209813287860733969412',
'81142660418086830619328460811191061556940512689692',
'51934325451728388641918047049293215058642563049483',
'62467221648435076201727918039944693004732956340691',
'15732444386908125794514089057706229429197107928209',
'55037687525678773091862540744969844508330393682126',
'18336384825330154686196124348767681297534375946515',
'80386287592878490201521685554828717201219257766954',
'78182833757993103614740356856449095527097864797581',
```

```
'1672632010043689784255353992093183744149780686 0984',
'4840309812907779179908821879532736447567559084 8030',
'8708698755139271185451707854416185242432069315 0332',
'5995940689575653678210707492696653767632623544 7210',
'6979395067965269474259770973916669376304263398 7085',
'4105268470829908521139942736573411618276031500 1271',
'6537860736150108085700914993951255702819874600 4375',
'3582903531743471732693212357815498262974255273 7307',
'9495375976510530594696606768315657437716740187 5275',
'8890280257173322961917666871381993181104877019 0271',
'2526768027607800301367868099252546340106163286 6526',
'3627021854049770558562994658063623799314074625 5962',
'2407448690823117497779236546625724692332281091 7141',
'9143028819710328859780666976089293863828502533 3403',
'3441306557801612781592181500556186883646842009 0470',
'2305308117281643048762379196984248725503663878 4583',
'1148769693215490281042402013833512446218144177 3470',
'6378329949063625966649858761822122522551248676 4533',
'6772018697169854431241957240991395900895231005 8822',
'9554825530026352078153229679624948164195386821 8774',
'7608532713228572311042480345612486769706450799 5236',
'3777424253541129168427686553892620502491032657 2967',
'2370191327572567528565324825826546309220705859 6522',
'2979886027225833191312637514734199488953476574 5501',
'1849570145487928898485682772607771372140379887 9715',
'3829820378303147352772158034814451349137322665 1381',
'3482954382919991818027891652243102739225112286 9539',
'4095795306640523263253804410005965493915987959 3635',
'2974615218550237130764225512118369380358038858 4903',
'4169811622207297718615823667842468915799353296 1922',
'6246795719440126904387710727504810239089552359 7457',
'2318970677254791506150550495392297953090112996 7519',
'8618808822587531452958409925120382900940777077 5672',
'1130673970830472448381653387350234084564705807 7308',
'8295917476714036319800818712901187549131054712 6581',
'9762333104481838626951545633492636657289756340 0500',
'4284628018351707052783183942588214552122725125 0327',
'5512160354698120058176216521282765275169129689 7789',
'3223819573432933994643750190783694576588335239 9886',
'7550616496518477518073816883786109152735792970 1337',
'6217784275219262340194239963916804498399317331 2731',
'3292418570714734956691667468763466091503591467 7504',
'9951867143023521962889489010242332511691361962 6622',
'7326746080059154747183079839286853520694694454 0724',
```

```
'7684182252467441716151403642798227334805555 6214818',
'9714261791034259864720451689398942217982608 8076852',
'8778364618279934631376775430780936333301898 2642090',
'1084880252167467088321512018588354322381287 6952786',
'7132961247478246453863699300904931036361976 3878039',
'6218407357239979422340623539380833965132740 8011116',
'6662789198148880779794187687614423003098449 0851411',
'6066182629368283676474477923918033511098906 9790714',
'8578694408955299065364044742557608365997664 5795096',
'6602439640990538960712019821997604759949019 7230297',
'6491398268003297315603712004137790378556608 5089252',
'1673093931987275027546890690370753941304265 2315011',
'9480937724504879515095410092164586375471059 8436791',
'7863916702118749243199570064191796977759902 8300699',
'1536871371193661495281130587638027841075444 9733078',
'4078992311553355625611423224232550336854424 88917353',
'4488991150144064802036906806396067232219320 4149535',
'4150312888033953605329934036800697710650566 631954',
'8123488067321014673905856855793458140362782 2703280',
'8261657077394832759223284594170652509451232 5230608',
'2291880205877731971983945018088807242966198 0811197',
'7715854250201654509041324580978688277894872 1859617',
'7210783843506918615543566288406225747369228 4509516',
'2084960398013400172393067166682355524525280 4609722',
'5350353422647252425087405407559178978126433 0331690'
);

var x: array[1..MN] of int; // sum
len: int; // len of the result

// returns the first (leftmost) index of x
function Carrying: int;
  var c, i, j, z: int;
begin
  c := 0; len := SLEN+2;
  j := len+1;
  for i := SLEN downto 1 do
  begin
    z := x[i]+c;
    dec(j);
    x[j] := z mod 10;
    c := z div 10;
  end;
  while (c > 0) do
```

```
begin
  dec(j);
  x[j] := c mod 10;
  c := c div 10;
end;
exit(j);
end; // Carrying

procedure E13;
var col, j, start, row: int;
begin
// Get the first row s[1], row = 1
row := 1;
for col := 1 to SLEN do
  x[col] := ord(s[row][ col])-ord('0');
// Sum of 100 input lines without carrying
for row := 2 to NUM do
  for col := 1 to SLEN do
  inc(x[col], ord(s[row][ col])-ord('0'));
start := Carrying;
write(NL, ' Start = ', start, ' Len = ', len);
write(NL,' Sum: ');
for col := start to len do write(x[col]);
write(NL,'  The First ten digits of the sum: ');
j := start + 9;
for col := start to j do write(x[col]);
write(NL, ' The  Last ten digits of the sum: ');
for col := len-9 to len do write(x[col]);
end; // E13

BEGIN
  E13;
  writeln(NL, '  T H E    E N D .');
  readln;
END.
```

Java Program

In the Java Program two variants are presented:

- Version e13A: direct adding.
- Version e13B: using BigInteger.

```java
/*********************************************************
   Problem 13. Large sum
   5537376230390876637302048746832985971773659831892672
   The First ten digits of the sum: 5537376230
   The Last ten digits of the sum: 9831892672
   Time = 0.02 sec.
*********************************************************/
import java.util.Arrays;
import java.math.*;
public class E13 {
private String[] s = {
"37107287533902102798797998220837590246510135740250",
"46376937677490009712648124896970078050417018260538",
"74324986199524741059474233309513058123726617309629",
"91942213363574161572522430563301811072406154908250",
"23067588207539346171171980310421047513778063246676",
"89261670696623363820136378418383684178734361726757",
"28112879812849979408065481931592621691275889832738",
"44274228917432520321923589422876796487670272189318",
"47451445736001306439091167216856844588711603153276",
"70386486105843025439939619828891759366568675793495 1",
"62176457141856560629502157223196586755079324193331",
"64906352462741904929101432445813822663347944758178",
"92575867718337217661963751590579239728245598838407",
"58203565325359399008402633568948830189458628227828",
"80181199384826282014278194139940567587151170094390",
"35398664372827112653829987240784473053190104293586",
"86515506006295864861532075273371959191420517255829",
"71693888707715466499115593487603532921714970056938",
"54370070576826684624621495650076471787294438377604",
"53282654108756828443191190634694037855217779295145",
"36123272525000296071075082563815656710885258350721",
"45876576172410976447339110607218265236877223636045",
"17423706905851860660448207621209813287860733969412",
"81142660418086830619328460811191061556940512689692",
"51934325451728388641918047049293215058642563049483",
"62467221648435076201727918039944693004732956340691",
"15732444386908125794514089057706229429197107928209",
"55037687525678773091862540744969844508330393682126",
"18336384825330154686196124348767681297534375946515",
"80386287592878490201521685554828717201219257766954",
"78182833757993103614740356856449095527097864797581",
"16726320100436897842553539920931837441497806860984",
"48403098129077791799088218795327364475675590848030",
```

```
"87086987551392711854517078544161852424320693150332",
"59959406895756536782107074926965376763262235447210",
"69793950679652694742597709739166693763042633987085",
"41052684708299085211399427365734116182760315001271",
"65378607361501080857009149939512557028198746004375",
"35829035317434717326932123578154982629742552737307",
"94953759765105305946966067683156574371167401875275",
"88902802571733229619176668713819931811048770190271",
"25267680276078003013678680992525463401061632866526",
"36270218540497705585629946580636237993140746255962",
"24074486908231174977792365466257246923322810917141",
"91430288197103288597806669760892938638285025333403",
"34413065578016127815921815005561868836468420090470",
"23053081172816430487623791969842487255036638784583",
"11487696932154902810424020138335124462181441773470",
"63783299490636259666498587618221225225512486764533",
"67720186971698544312419572409913959008952310058822",
"95548255300263520781532296796249481641953868218774",
"76085327132285723110424803456124867697064507995236",
"37774242535411291684276865538926205024910326572967",
"23701913275725675285653248258265463092207058596522",
"29798860272258331913126375147341994889534765745501",
"18495701454879288984856827726077713721403798879715",
"38298203783031473527721580348144513491373226651381",
"34829543829199918180278916522431027392251122869539",
"40957953066405232632538044100059654939159879593635",
"29746152185502371307642255121183693803580388584903",
"41698116222072977186158236678424689157993532961922",
"62467957194401269043877107275048102390895523597457",
"23189706772547915061505504953922979530901129967519",
"86188088225875314529584099251203829009407770775672",
"11306739708304724483816533873502340845647058077308",
"82959174767140363198008187129011875491310547126581",
"97623331044818386269515456334926366572897563400500",
"42846280183517070527831839425882145521227251250327",
"55121603546981200581762165212827652751691296897789",
"32238195734329339946437501907836945765883352399886",
"75506164965184775180738168837861091527357929701337",
"62177842752192623401942399639168044983993173312731",
"32924185707147349566916674687634660915035914677504",
"99518671430235219628894890102423325116913619626622",
"73267460800591547471830798392868535206946944540724",
"76841822524674417161514036427982273348055556214818",
"97142617910342598647204516893989422179826088076852",
```

Nguyen Xuan Huy | 112

```
    "87783646182799346313767754307809363333018982642090",
    "10848802521674670883215120185883543223812876952786",
    "71329612474782464538636993009049310363619763878039",
    "62184073572399794223406235393808339651327408011116",
    "66627891981488087797941876876144230030984490851411",
    "60661826293682836764744779239180335110989069790714",
    "85786944089552990653640447425576083659976645795096",
    "66024396409905389607120198219976047599490197230297",
    "64913982680032973156037120041377903785566085089252",
    "16730939319872750275468906903707539413042652315011",
    "94809377245048795150954100921645863754710598436791",
    "78639167021187492431995700641917969777599028300699",
    "15368713711936614952811305876380278410754449733078",
    "40789923115535562561142322423255033685442488917353",
    "44889911501440648020369068063960672322193204149535",
    "41503128880339536053299340368006977710650566631954",
    "81234880673210146739058568557934581403627822703280",
    "82616570773948327592232845941706525094512325230608",
    "22918802058777319719839450180888072429661980811197",
    "77158542502016545090413245809786882778948721859617",
    "72107838435069186155435662884062257473692284509516",
    "20849603980134001723930671666823555245252804609722",
    "53503534226472524250874054075591789781264330331690"
    };

    private int MN = 52;
    private int LEN = 50;
    private int NUM = 100;
    private int[] x = new int[MN];
    private int len = 0;

    E13() {
      e13A();
      e13B();
    }

    // Variant A: Direct Adding
    private void e13A() {
      int col, j, row, start;
      // Get the first row s[0]
      row = 1;
      for (col = 0; col < LEN; ++col)
        x[col] = s[0].charAt(col)-'0';
        // Sum of 100 input lines without carrying
```

```
  for (row = 1; row < NUM; ++row)
    for (col = 0; col < LEN; ++col)
      x[col] += (s[row].charAt(col)-'0');
  start = carrying();
  System.out.print("\n Method A: \n Sum: ");
  for (col = start; col <= len; ++col)
    System.out.print(x[col]);
  // Print 10 digits
System.out.print("\nThe First ten digits of the sum:");
j = start+10;
for (col = start; col < j; ++col)
  System.out.print(x[col]);
System.out.print("\nThe Last ten digits of the sum: ");
start = len-9;
for (col = start; col <= len; ++col)
  System.out.print(x[col]);
} // e13A

// returns the first (leftmost) index of x
private int carrying() {
  int c, i, j, z;
  c = 0;
  len = LEN+1;
  for (i = LEN-1, j = len; i >= 0; --i, --j) {
    z = x[i]+c;
    x[j] = z % 10;
    c = z / 10;
  } // for
  while (c > 0) {
    x[j--] = c % 10;
    c /= 10;
  } // while
  return j+1;
} // carrying

// Method B: Use BigInteger
private void e13B() {
  BigInteger x = new BigInteger(s[0]);
  for (int i = 1; i < NUM; ++i)
    x = x.add(new BigInteger(s[i]));
  System.out.print("\n\n Method B: " + x);
  String snum = x.toString();
System.out.print("\nThe First ten digits of the sum:");
for (int i = 0; i < 10; ++i)
```

```
  System.out.print(snum.charAt(i));
System.out.print("\nThe  Last ten digits of the sum:");
int len = snum.length();
for (int i  = len-10;  i < len; ++i)
  System.out.print(snum.charAt(i));
} // e13B
} // class E13
```

Problem 14. Longest Collatz sequence

The following iterative sequence is defined for the set of positive integers:

$n \rightarrow n/2$ (n is even)

$n \rightarrow 3n + 1$ (n is odd)

Using the rule above and starting with 13, we generate the following sequence:

$13 \rightarrow 40 \rightarrow 20 \rightarrow 10 \rightarrow 5 \rightarrow 16 \rightarrow 8 \rightarrow 4 \rightarrow 2 \rightarrow 1$.

It can be seen that this sequence (starting at 13 and finishing at 1) contains 10 terms. Although it has not been proved yet (Collatz Problem), it is thought that all starting numbers finish at 1.

Which starting number, under one million, produces the longest chain?

NOTE: Once the chain starts the terms are allowed to go above one million.

Algorithm

Let $C(n) = (c_1 = n) \rightarrow c_2 \rightarrow \ldots \rightarrow (c_m = 1)$ be the Collatz sequence starting with $n \geq 1$. Denote by $\#C(n)$ the length (number of terms) of $C(n)$, $\#C(n) = m$ and for each term c_i in $C(n)$, denote by $Pos(c_i, n) = i$.

Notes

R1. For any $n \geq 1$, all terms in $C(n)$ are different. This note is not proved yet because the Collatz conjecture has not been proved for any n. But we can test $C(n)$ for n about some billions, that is enought for the given problem.

R2. If x is in $C(n)$ then $\#C(n) = \#C(x) + Pos(x, n) - 1$. Inded, let

$C(n) = c_1 \rightarrow \ldots \rightarrow c_k = x \rightarrow \ldots \rightarrow c_m = 1$. Then we have

$c_k = x$

$\#C(n) = m$

$Pos(x, n) = k$

$\#C(x) = \#C(c_k) = m - k + 1 = m - Pos(x, n) + 1$

Hence,

$$\#C(n) = m = (m - k + 1) + k - 1 = \#C(x) + Pos(x, n) - 1$$

Following R2, if we get such term c_i in the chain $C(n)$ that $\#C(c_i)$ is known before, then we can immediately set $\#C(n) = \#C(c_i) + i - 1$ and break the chain at this point. Therefore, for each $n = 1, 2, \ldots$, we try to calculate and save the length of terms x in $C(n)$ to an array len[], where len$[x] = \#C(x)$.

We know that $C(1) = 1$ so, len$[1] = \#C(1) = 1$. Then we calculate all len$[n] = \#C(n)$, $2 \le n \le 999999$. For example, if all len$[n]$, $1 \le n \le 6$ are computed, and we need compute len[7].

n	1	2	3	4	5	6	7
len(n)	1	2	8	3	6	9	?

We have,

i	1	2	3	4	5	6	7	8	9	10	11	12	...
$C(7)$ c_i	7	22	11	34	17	52	26	13	40	20	10	5	...

$Pos(5, 7) = 12$ and before, we know len$[5] = 6$, hence we set len$[7] = $ len$[5] + Pos(5, 7) - 1 = 6 + 12 - 1 = 17$.

The following example demonstrates how to get len$[n]$, $1 \le n \le 10$.

Example

C(1) = 1, len[1] = 1.
C(2) = 2 → **1**. len[2] = 2.
C(3) = 3 → 10 → 5 → 16 → 8 → 4 → **2**... pos(2,3) = 7.
So, len[3] = len[2] + 7 − 1 = 8.
C(4) = 4 → **2** ... pos(2,4) = 2. So, len[4] = len[2] + 2 − 1 = 3.
C(5) = 5, 16, 8, **4**... pos(4,5) = 4. So, len[5] = len[4] + 4 − 1 = 6.
C(6) = 6, **3**... pos(3,6) = 2. So, len[6] = len[3] + 2 − 1 = 9.
C(7) = 7 → 22 → 11 → 34 → 17 → 52 → 26 → 13 → 40 → 20 → 10 → **5**...

pos(5,7) = 12. So, len[7] = len[5] + 12 − 1 = 17.
C(8) = 8 → **4** ... pos(4,8) = 2. So, len[8] = len[4] + 2 − 1 = 4.
C(9) = 9 → 28 → 14 → **7** ... pos(7,9) = 4. So, len[9] = len[7] + 4 − 1 = 20.
C(10) = 10 → **5**... pos(5,10) = 2. So, len[10] = len[5] + 2 − 1 = 7.

Note

Because the terms of generated Collatz sequence can be very large, integer type of 64 bits is recommended in the programs.

C++ Program

```
/*********************************************
   Problem 14. Longest Collatz sequence
   Version E14A
   Answer = 837799 (Maxlen = 525)
   Time = 0.06 sec.
*********************************************/
#include <iostream>
#include <windows.h>

using namespace std;

typedef unsigned long long UL;

const int MN = 1000000;
int len[MN];

// Generate Collatz sequence with start value n
// len[n] = len[x]+Pos(x,n)-1, x < n
void Collatz(int n) {
  UL x = n;
  int pos = 1;
  while (x >= n) {
    ++pos;
    x = (x & 1) ? 3*x + 1 :  x >>= 1;
  } // while
  // x < n
  len[n] = len[x] + pos - 1;
} // Collatz

void E14A() {
  int i, imax;
```

```
  len[1] = 1;
  for (i = 2; i < MN; ++i)
    Collatz(i);
  // get max len
  imax = 1;
  for (i = 2; i < MN; ++i)
    if (len[i] > len[imax])  imax = i;
  cout << "\n Result: Start number = " << imax;
  cout << "\n Max len = " << len[imax];
} // E14A

main() {
  E14A(); // 837799 525
  cout << "\n  T H E   E N D .";
  return 0;
}
```

Free Pascal Program

```
(*****************************************
   Problem 14. Longest Collatz sequence
   Version E14A
   Answer: 837799 (Maxlen = 525)
   Time = 0.06 sec.
*****************************************)
const NL = #13#10; MN = 1000000;
type int = longint;
var  len: array[1..MN] of int;

// Generate Collatz sequence with start value n
// len[n] = len[x]+Pos(x,n)-1, x < n
procedure Collatz(n: int);
  var x: int64;
  pos: int;
begin
  x := n; pos := 1;
  while x >= n do
  begin
    inc(pos);
    if Odd(x) then x := 3*x + 1 else x := x shr 1;
  end; // while
  len[n] := len[x] + pos - 1;
end; // Collatz
```

```
procedure E14A;
  var i, imax: int;
begin
  len[1] := 1;
  for i := 2 to MN-1 do
    Collatz(i);
  // Get max len
  imax := 1;
  for i:= 2 to MN-1 do
    if (len[i] > len[imax])  then imax := i;
  writeln(NL, ' Result: Start number = ', imax);
  writeln(' Max len = ', len[imax]);
end; // E14A

BEGIN
  E14A; // 837799 525
  writeln(' T H E   E N D . ');
  readln;
END.
```

Java Program

```
/*********************************
   Problem 14. Longest Collatz
   Version E14A
   Answer: 837799 (Maxlen = 525)
   Time = 0.06 sec.
*********************************/
import java.util.Arrays;

public class E14 {
  private static int MN = 1000000;
  private static int EXP = 20;
   private static int[] len = new int[MN];
    E14() {
      E14A();
    } // E14

   private void E14A() {
    len[1] = 1;
    for (int n = 2; n < MN; ++n)
      collatz(n);
    // Get max len
```

```
int imax = 1;
for (int i = 2; i < MN; ++i)
  if (len[i] > len[imax])  imax = i;
System.out.println("\n Result: Start number = "
      + imax);
System.out.println(" Max len = " + len[imax]);
} // E14A

// Generate Collatz sequence with start value n
// len[n] = len[x]+Pos(x,n)-1, x < n
private void collatz(int n) {
  int pos = 1;
  long x = n;
  while (x >= n) {
    ++pos;
    x = ((x & 1) != 0) ? 3*x + 1 : (x >> 1);
  } // while
  len[n] = len[(int)x] + pos - 1;
} // collatz
} // class E14
```

Enhancement

In the first step, you can calculate many values of the len[n]. For example, following the definition of the Collatz sequence, we know that len[2^i] = $i+1$, and it is easy to compute 2^i by left shifting 1 to i bit-positions,

$2^i = 1$ shift left i.

len[2^i] = $i + 1$, $0 \le i \le 19$

Note that, $2^0 = 1$, and $2^{19} = 524288 < 1000000$ but $2^{20} = 1048576 > 1000000$.

i	0	1	2	3	4	5	...	19
2^i	1	2	4	8	16	32	...	524288
len(2^i)	1	2	3	4	5	6	...	20

In general, if we know len[y] for some y then we can set len[$y2^k$] = len[y] + k. For example, if we know len[3] = 8 then we can set len[6] = 9, len[12] = 10, len[24] = 11, ...

Let $C(n) = c_1 \rightarrow \ldots \rightarrow c_i \rightarrow \ldots \rightarrow c_m = 1$. Then we have

    len[n] = m.

    len[c_i] = $m - i + 1$ = len[n] $-$ pos(c_i, n) + 1.

    len[$2^k c_i$] = len[c_i] + k = $m - i + k + 1$ = len[n] $-$ pos(c_i, n) + k + 1,

    $1 \leq i \leq m$.

The above equalities show that, if we know len[n], then we can get len[x] for all x in $C(n)$. Hence, we try to save pos(x, n) for all terms x when generating Collatz chain $C(n)$.

The following example demonstrates how to get len[n], $1 \leq n \leq 10$ by the new approach.

Example

(1)   Initialize: Set len[2^i] = i+1, $0 \leq i \leq 19$.

(2)   len[2] = 2 Is done in (1).

(3)   len[3] = ?. C(3) = 3 → 10 → 5 → **16**. len[16] = 5 is done in (1).
       So, len[3] = len[16] + pos(16, 3) − 1 = 5 + 4 − 1 = 8.
       Now we conculate len[$y2^k$] for all y in the prefix chain C(3): 5, 10, 3.
       len[5] = len[3]−3+1 = 6, len[10] = 7, len[20] = 8, len[40] = 9, ...;
       len[6] = len[3] + 1 = 9, len[12] = 10, ...

(4)   len[4] = 3 is done in (1).

(5)   len[5] = 6 is done in (3).

(6)   len[6] = 9 is done in (3)

(7)   len[7] = ?. C(7) = 7 → 22 → 11 → 34 → 17 → 52 → 26 → 13 → **40**. len[40] = 9 is done in (3).
       So, len[7] = len[40] + pos(40, 7) − 1 = 9 + 9 − 1 = 17.
       Now we calculate len[$y2^k$] for all y in prefix chain C(7): 7, 11, 17, 13.

(8)   len[8] = 4 is done in (1).

(9)   len[9] = ?. C(9) = 9 → **28**. len[28] = 19 is done in (7), pos(28, 9) = 2.
       So len[9] = 19 + 2 − 1 = 20.

(10)   len[10] = 7 is done in (3).

We also see that if $n = 2k$ then $k < n$ and len[k] is computed before n, hence len[n] = len[k]+1. Therefore, we need only to calculate len[n] for all odd numbers n.

The following algorithm E14B solves the problem by the new approach.

```
Algorithm E14B
Input: MN = 1000000
Output: integer n | #C(n) = max {#C(i) | 1 ≤ i < MN}.
begin
    Set len[1] ← 1;
    Set len[2^i] ← i+1, 2 ≤ 2^i < MN;
    Set all rest len[i] ← 0;
    for each odd n ← 3 to MN−1 do
        if (len[n] = 0) then Collatz(n) endif;
    endfor
    return n where len[n] = max {len[i] | 1 ≤ i < MN}
endE14B
```

The Collatz algorithm below calculates the lengths of all terms y and $y2^k$ in Collatz chain $C(n)$.

```
Algorithm Collatz
Input: MN = 1000000
       odd integer n < MN
Output: len[n]
begin
    pos ← 1;
    x ← n;
    if (n = 1) then return 1 endif;
    while (true) do
        pos ← pos + 1;
        if (x is odd) then   x ← (3 × x) + 1
            else x ← x div 2
        endif;
        if (x < MN) then
            if (len[x] > 0) breakwhile endif
            // x < MN and len[x] = 0
```

```
        save (x, pos) to stack (ss, pp);
      endif x < MN
    endwhile
    len[n] ← len[x] + pos - 1;
    calculate len[n×2^k] = len[n]+k for all n×2^k < MN
    for each y in ss  do
        len[y] ← len[n] - pp[y] + 1;
        calculate len[y×2^k] = len[y]+k for all y×2^k < MN
    endfor
    return len[n];
  endCollatz
```

C++ Program

```cpp
/*****************************************
   Problem 14. Longest Collatz sequence
   Version E14B.
   Answer = 837799 (Maxlen = 525)
   Time = 0.05 sec.
*****************************************/
#include <iostream>
#include <windows.h>

using namespace std;

typedef unsigned long long UL;

const int MN = 1000000;
int len[MN];
int ss[MN]; // stack for saving x
int pp[MN]; // stack for saving positions
int ii; // index for ss, pp

// Generate Collatz sequence with start value n
// len[n] = len[x]+Pos(x,n)-1, x < n
void Collatz(UL n) {
  int pos = 1, i;
  UL x = n;
  int y, leny;
  // Put (n, 1) to stacks ss, pp
  ii = 1; ss[ii] = x; pp[ii] = pos;
  if (n == 1) return;
  while (true) {
```

```
    ++pos; // new term at pos
    x = (x & 1) ? 3*x + 1 :  (x >> 1);
    if (x < MN) {
      if (len[x] > 0) break;
      // x < MN and len[x] = 0
      // put (x, pos) to stacks ss, pp
      ++ii; ss[ii] = x; // save x
      pp[ii] = pos; // save position of x
    } // if x < MN
  } // while
  len[n] = len[x] + pos - 1;
  // len[n*2^k] = len[n] + k
  y = (n << 1); leny = len[n] + 1;
  while (y < MN && len[y] == 0) {
    len[y] = leny;
    y <<= 1; ++leny;
  } // while
  // Compute len[y], y in stack
  for (i = ii; i > 0; --i) {
    y = ss[i];
    if (len[y] == 0) {
      len[y] = len[n] - pp[i] + 1;
      // len[y*2^k] = len[y] + k;
      leny = len[y] + 1;
      y <<= 1; // x = 2x
      while (y < MN && len[y] == 0) {
        len[y] = leny;
        y <<= 1; ++leny;
      } // while y < MN
    } // if len[y] == 0
  } // for i
}// Collatz

void E14B() {
  int i, j, imax;
  // Init all len[i] = 0, 1 <= i <= 999999
  // for (i = 1; i < MN; ++i) len[i] = 0;
  memset(len, 0, sizeof(len));
  len[1] = 1;
  // len(2^i) = i+1
  // 524288 = 2^19 < 1000000
  j = 1;
  for (i = 1; i <= 19; ++i) {
    j <<= 1; // j = 2*j = 2^(i)
```

```
    len[j] = i+1;
  } // for
  for (i = 3; i < MN; i += 2)
    if (len[i] == 0) Collatz(i);

// get max len
imax = 1;
for (i = 2; i < MN; ++i)
  if (len[i] > len[imax])  imax = i;
   cout << "\n Result: Start number = " << imax;
   cout << "\n Max len = " << len[imax];
 } // E14B

  main() {
    E14B(); // 837799 525
    cout << "\n  T H E   E N D .";
    return 0;
  }
```

Pascal Program

```
(****************************************
   Problem 14. Longest Collatz sequence
   Version E14B.
   Answer = 837799 (Maxlen = 525)
   Time = 0.05 sec.
****************************************)

const MN = 1000000;
NL = #13#10;
type int = longint;
ArrayType = array[1..MN] of int;
var
   len,
   ss, // stack for saving x
   pp : ArrayType; // stack for saving pos of x
   ii: int; // index for ss, pp

// Generate Collatz sequence with start value n
// len[n] = len[x]+Pos(x,n)-1, x < n
procedure Collatz(n: int64);
  var i, pos, leny: int;
  x: int64;
  y : int;
```

```
begin
  pos := 1;
  x := n;
  if (n = 1) then exit;
  // put (n, 1) to stacks ss and pp
  ii := 1; ss[ii] := n; pp[ii] := pos;
  while (true) do
  begin
    inc(pos);
    if odd(x) then x := x*3 + 1
      else x := x div 2;
    if (x < MN) then
    begin
      if (len[x] > 0) then break;
      // x < MN and len[x] := 0
      // put (x, pos) to stacks ss, pp
      inc(ii); ss[ii] := x; // save x to ss
      pp[ii] := pos; // save position of x to pp
    end; // if x < MN
  end; // while
  len[n] := len[x] + pos - 1;
  // len[n*2^i] = len[n]+i
  y := (n shl 1); // y = 2n
  leny := len[n] + 1;
  while (y <= MN) and (len[y] = 0) do
  begin
    len[y] := leny;
    inc(leny); y := y shl 1;
  end; // while y
  // pop from stacks
  for i := ii downto 1 do
  begin
    y := ss[i];
    if (len[y] = 0) then
    begin
      len[y] := len[n] - pp[i] + 1;
      leny := len[y] + 1;
      y := y shl 1;
      while (y <= MN) and (len[y] = 0) do
      begin
        len[y] := leny;
        inc(leny); y := y shl 1;
      end;  // while
    end; // if
```

```
  end; // for
end; // Collatz

procedure E14B;
  var i, j, imax: int;
begin
  // Init all len[i] := 0, 1 <:= i <:= 999999
  for i := 1 to MN-1 do len[i] := 0;
  len[1] := 1;
  // len(2^k) := k+1
  // 524288 := 2^19 < 1000000
  j := 1;
  for i := 1 to 19 do
  begin
    j := j shl 1; len[j] := i+1;
  end; // for
  i := 3;
  while (i < MN) do
  begin
    if (len[i] = 0) then Collatz(i);
    inc(i, 2);
  end; // while
  // get max len
imax := 1;
  for i := 2 to MN-1 do
    if (len[i] > len[imax]) then imax := i;
  writeln(NL, ' Result: Start number = ', imax);
  writeln(NL, ' Max len = ', len[imax]);
end; // E14B

BEGIN
  E14B; // 837799 525
  writeln(NL, '  T H E   E N D .');
  readln;
END.
```

Java Program

```
/******************************************
   Problem 14. Longest Collatz
   Version E14A
   Answer: 837799 (Maxlen = 525)
   Time = 0.05 sec.
 ******************************************/
```

```java
import java.util.Arrays;

public class E14 {
    private static int MN = 1000000;
    private static int[] len = new int[MN];
    private static int[] ss = new int[MN];
    // stack for saving x
    private static int[] pp = new int[MN];
    // stack for saving pos of x
    private static int ii; // index of stacks ss and pp

    E14() {
        E14B();
    } // E14

    private void E14B() {
        int i, j, imax;
        // Init all len[i] = 0, 1 <= i <= 999999
        for (i = 1; i < MN; ++i) len[i] = 0;
        len[1] = 1;
        // len(2^k) = k+1
        // 524288 = 2^19 < 1000000
        j = 1;
        for (i = 1; i <= 19; ++i) {
            j <<= 1; len[j] = i+1;
        } // for
        for (i = 3; i < MN; i += 2)
            if (len[i] == 0) Collatz(i);
        // get max len
        imax = 1;
        for (i = 2; i < MN; ++i)
            if (len[i] > len[imax])  imax = i;
        System.out.println("\n Result: Start number = "
                + imax);
        System.out.println(" Max len = " + len[imax]);
    } // E14B

    // Generate Collatz sequence with start value n
    // len[n] = len[x]+Pos(x,n)-1, x < n
    private void Collatz(int n) {
        int pos = 1, i, ix;
        int y, leny;
        long x = n;
        if (n == 1) return;
```

```
    ii = 0;
    while (true) {
      ++pos;
      x = ((x & 1) == 1) ? 3*x + 1 :  (x >> 1);
      // if (x >= MN) continue;
      if (x < (long)MN) {
          ix = (int)x;
          if (len[ix] > 0) break;
          // x < MN and len[x] = 0
          // save x
          ++ii; ss[ii] = ix;
          pp[ii] = pos; // save position of x
      } // if x < MN
    } // while
    len[n] = len[ix] + pos - 1;
    y = (n << 1); // y = 2x
    // len[y*2^k] = len[y] + k
    leny = len[n] + 1;
    while (y < MN && len[y] == 0) {
      len[y] = leny;
      y <<= 1; ++leny;
    } // while
    // pop from stack ss, pp
    for (i = 1; i <= ii; ++i){
      y = ss[i];
      len[y] = len[n] - pp[i] + 1;
      leny = len[y] + 1; y <<= 1;
      while (y < MN && len[y] == 0) {
          len[y] = leny;
          ++leny; y <<= 1;
      } // while
    } // for
  } // Collatz
} // class E14
```

Problem 15. Lattice paths

Starting in the top left corner of a 2×2 grid, there are 6 routes (without backtracking) to the bottom right corner.

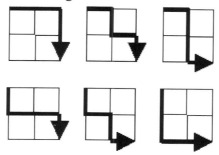

How many routes are there through a 20×20 grid?

Algorithm

We try to solve a more general problem with a grid $a \times b$, where a is the height and b is the width of the grid. First, we call a path without backtracking from A to C a *legal path*. In the grid, we label 0 to the horizontal edge, and 1 to the vertical edge.

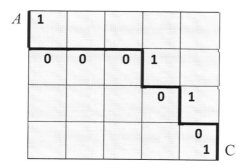

Path 100010101 in the 4×5
grid. a = 4, b = 5.

We see that all legal paths must go through exactly a vertical edges and exactly b horizontal edges. This implies that all legal paths have length $a+b$. Hence the problem can be formulated as follows.

How many binary strings of length $a+b$ having exactly a symbols 1 (or b symbols 0).

The answer will be $\binom{n}{k}$ - the *k-combination* of n, and has formula

$$\binom{n}{k} = \frac{n!}{k!\,(n-k)!} = \frac{n(n-1)\cdots(n-k+1)}{k(k-1)\cdots 1}$$

where $0! = 1$, $n = a+b$, $k = a$ (or $k = b$).

For example, six legal paths in the given 2×2 grid will be

0011, 0101, 0110, 1001, 1010, 1100.

We have

$$\binom{n}{k} = \frac{n!}{k!\,(n-k)!} = \frac{n!}{(k-1)!\,(n-k+1)!} \times \frac{n-k+1}{k}$$
$$= \binom{n}{k-1} \times \frac{n-k+1}{k}$$

We now use the linear notation $C(n, k)$ for the *k-combination* of n. Then we have

$C(n, k) = C(n, k-1)(n-k+1)$ div k (15.1)

$C(n, 0) = 1$.

$C(n, 1) = n$.

A recursive version for $C(n, k)$ is

    $C(n, k) =$ if $(k = 1)$ then return n else return $(C(n, k-1) \times (n-k+1))$ div k.

Replacing k in (15.1) by $i+1$ we get

$C(n, i+1) = C(n, i)(n-i)$ div $(i+1)$ (15.2)

In the non-recursive form, using (15.2), the function $C(n, k)$ looks like this

Algorithm C(n, k)
Input: positive integers n , k.
Output: k-combination of n
begin
r ← 1; // r = C(n, 0)
for i ← 0 to k-1 do
r = (r × (n-i)) div (i+1);
// C(n, i+1) = C(n, i)(n-i) div (i+1)
endfor
return r;
endC(k, n)

C++ Program

```
/ * * * * * * * * * * * * * * * * * * * * * * * * * * * * * * * * * * * * * * * * * * *
   Problem 15. Lattice paths
   Answer = 137846528820, Time = 0.02 sec.
* * * * * * * * * * * * * * * * * * * * * * * * * * * * * * * * * * * * * * * * * * * */

#include <iostream>

using namespace std;

typedef unsigned long long UL;

// Recursive of C(n, k)
UL RC(UL n, UL k) {
  return (k == 1) ? n : RC(n,k-1)*(n-k+1)/k;
} // RC

// non recursive of C(n, k)
UL C(UL n, UL k) {
  UL r = 1;
  for (int i = 0; i < k; ++i) {
    r = r * (n-i) / (i+1);
  } // for
  return r;
} // C

main() {
  int n = 20;
  cout << RC(n+n, n); // 137846528820
  cout << endl << C(n+n, n); // 137846528820
```

```cpp
  cout << "\n  T H E   E N D .";
  return 0;
}
```

Free Pascal Program

```pascal
(********************************************
  Problem 15. Lattice paths
  Answer = 137846528820, Time = 0.02 sec.
*********************************************)

const NL = #13#10;

// recursive of C(n, k)
function RC(n, k: word): int64;
begin
  if (k = 0) then exit(1)
    else exit(RC(n,k-1)*(n-k+1) div k);
end; // RC

// non recursive of C(n, k)
function C(n, k: word): int64;
  var r: int64;
  i: word;
begin
  r := 1;
  for i := 0 to k-1 do
    r := r * (n-i) div (i+1);
  exit(r);
end; // C

BEGIN
  writeln(NL, RC(40,20)); // 137846528820
  writeln(NL, C(40,20)); // 137846528820
  writeln(NL, '  T H E   E N D .');
  readln;
END.
```

Java Program

```java
/*********************************************
  Problem 15. Lattice paths
  Answer = 137846528820, Time = 0.02 sec.
*********************************************/
```

```
public class E15 {
  private int n = 20;

  E15(){
   System.out.println(RC(n+n, n));
   System.out.println(C(n+n, n));
  }

  // Recursive of C(n, k)
  private long RC(long n, long k) {
   return (k == 1) ? n : RC(n,k-1)*(n-k+1)/k;
  } // RC

  // non Recursive of C(n, k)
  private long C(int n, int k) {
   long r = 1;
   for (int i = 0; i < k; ++i) {
    r = r * (n-i) / (i+1);
   } // for
   return r;
  } // C
} // class E15
```

Problem 16. Power digit sum

$2^{15} = 32768$ and the sum of its digits is $3 + 2 + 7 + 6 + 8 = 26$.

What is the sum of the digits of the number 2^{1000}?

Algorithm

This problem requests a technique of the big number representation.

```
Algorithm E15
Input: MN = 1000
Output: sum of digits of 2^MN.
begin
    x ← 1;
    for i ← 2 to MN do
        x ← x × 2;
    endfor
    return (sum of digits of x);
endE15
```

We represent a big unsigned integer by an array x[] in reversed form with the number of digits len. For example, number $x = 2^{13} = 8192$ is represented as follows,

Position	0	1	2	3
x	2	9	1	8

len(x) = 4

After multiplying 2^{13} by 2 we get $2^{14} = 2 \times 8192 = 16384$.

Position	0	1	2	3	4
x	4	8	3	6	1

len(x) = 5

Note

In the computer, the integers are represented in the binary form, hence, for the efficiency, we will use bit operations instead arithmetic operations. Some important replacements are the following.

	$a \times 2^k$	$a \ div \ 2^k$	$a \ mod \ 2^k$
	a shift left k	a shift right k	a and (2^k-1)
C++, Java	a << k	a >> k	a & (2^k-1)
Pascal	a shl k	a shr k	a AND (2^k-1)

Examples

Actions	C++	Pascal	Java	Comment
Initialize	int a=3,z=0;	a,z: integer;	int a=3,z=0;	
$a \leftarrow 3; z \leftarrow 0;$		a:=3; z:=0;		a=3; z=0;
$z \leftarrow a \times 2^{10}$	z = (a<<10);	z := a shl 10;	z = (a<<10);	z = 3072
$z \leftarrow z \ div \ 2^8$	z >>= 8;	z := z shr 8;	z >>= 8;	z = 12
$a \leftarrow z \ mod \ 8$	a = z & 7;	a := z and 7;	a = z & 7;	a = 4

If d is a digits, then $d*2 \le 9*2 = 18$, so the maximum carry of $d*2$ is 1.

C++ Program

```
/**********************************************
Problem 16. Power digit sum
Answer = 1366, Time = 0.02 sec.
*********************************************/

#include <iostream>
#include <windows.h>
#include <math.h>

using namespace std;

const int MN = 1000;

char x[500];
int len; // number of digits
```

```
// x = x * 2;
void Mult2() {
  char c = 0; // c is carry
  for (int i = 0; i < len; ++i) {
    x[i] = (x[i] << 1) + c; //x[i]=x[i]*2+c
    c = 1;
    if (x[i] >= 10) x[i] -= 10;
    else c = 0;
  } // for
  if (c > 0) x[len++] = c;
} // Mult2

void E16() {
  int i, sum;
  len = 1;
  x[0] = 1;
  for (i = 0; i < MN; ++i) Mult2();
  sum = 0;
  for (i = 0; i < len; ++i)  sum += x[i];
  cout << sum;
} // E16

main() {
  E16(); // 1366
  cout << "\n  T H E    E N D .";
  return 0;
}
```

Free Pascal Program

```
(***********************************
  Problem 16. Power digit sum
  Answer = 1366, Time = 0.02 sec.
***********************************)
const MN = 1000;
type int = integer;
var
  x: array[1..500] of byte;
  len: int;
// x = x * 2;
procedure Mult2;
  var i: int;
  c: byte;
```

```
begin
  c := 0; // the carry
  for i := 1 to len do
  begin
    x[i] := (x[i] shl 1) + c; // *2
    c := 1;
    if (x[i] >= 10) then x[i] := x[i] - 10 else c := 0;
  end; // for
  if (c > 0) then
  begin
    inc(len);
    x[len] := c;
  end; // if
end; // Mult2

procedure E16;
  var i, sum: int;
begin
  len := 1; x[1] := 1;
  for i := 1 to MN do Mult2;
  sum := 0;
  for i := 1 to len do sum := sum + x[i];
  writeln(sum);
end; // E16

BEGIN
  E16; // 1366
  writeln(' T H E    E N D .');
  readln;
END.
```

Java Program

In the Java Program two variants are presented:

- Variant e16A: direct adding.
- Variant e16B: using BigInteger.

```
/**********************************
Problem 16. Power digit sum
Answer = 1366, Time = 0.02 sec.
**********************************/
```

```java
import java.math.*;

public class E16 {
private static int MN = 1000;
private int[] x;
private int len = 0; // The length of x

E16()  {
  System.out.println("\n E16A: " + e16A());
  System.out.println("\n E16B: " + e16B());
}

private int e16A() {
  BigInteger n = new BigInteger("1");
  String s = (n.shiftLeft(MN)).toString();
  int sum = 0;
  for (int i = 0; i < s.length(); i++) {
  sum += (int)s.charAt(i)-'0';
  } // for
  return sum;
} // e16A

private int e16B() {
  int sum = 0;
  len = 1; // The length of x
  x = new int[500];
  x[0] = 1;
  for (int i = 0; i < MN; ++i) mult2();
  for (int i = 0; i < len; ++i) sum += x[i];
  return sum;
} // e16B

// x = x * 2
private void mult2() {
  int c = 0; // carry
  for (int i = 0; i < len; ++i) {
  x[i] = (x[i] << 1) + c;
  c = 1;
  if (x[i] >= 10) x[i] -= 10; else c = 0;
  } // for
  if (c > 0) { x[len] = c; ++len; }
} // mult2
} // class E16
```

Comment

Since function Mult2 in the given programs calculates $x = 2 \times x$ for each time, the loop number needed will be 1000. If we calculate $x = x \times 2^k$, with $m \times k = 1000$ for some k and m then the loop number can be reduced to m. This tells us to choose k as a factor of 1000, for example 1, 2, 4, 10, 20 or 25. In the other hand, we know that $x \times 2^k = x$ shift left k, so we need use an integer type of x enough larger than k bits, for example `int` (in C++ and Java, 4 bytes = 32 bits) and `longint` (in Pascal, 4 bytes = 32 bits). It is better if the bit-size of x is greater than $2k$. If we choose $k = 25$, then $x \times 2^{25}$ is equivalent to x shift left 25 = $x \times 33554432$. This product will be done with one shift left, hence the product 2^{1000} can be done after 1000 div 25 = 40 times of shift left. We do not choose $k > 25$ because in this case (x shift left k) may results a value-over. The algorithm ShiftLeft(k) for calculating $x = x \times 2^k$ now has the following form.

```
Algorithm ShiftLeft
Input: integer k is a factor of 1000.
Output: x ← x × 2^k.
begin
    carry ← 0;
    len ← length(x);
    for i ← 1 to len do
        x[i] ← (x[i] shift left k) + carry;
        carry ← x[i] div 10;
        x[i] ← x[i] − carry × 10;
    endfor
    while (carry ≠ 0) do
        len ← len + 1;
        d ← carry div 10;
        x[len] ← carry − (d × 10);
        carry ← d;
    endwhile
    Set length(x) ← len;
endShiftLeft.
```

Now, the algorithm for solving Problem 16 by the new approach is presented as follows.

Algorithm E16B
Input: MN = 1000.
integer k is a factor of MN.
Output: sum of digits of 2^{MN}.
begin
Set x[1] ← 1;
for i ← 1 to (MN div k) do
ShiftLeft(k);
sum ← 0;
for i ← 1 to length(x) do
sum ← sum + x[i];
endfor
return sum;
endE16B

C++ Program

```
/*****************************************
   Problem 16. Power digit sum
   Version 16B
   Answer = 1366, Time = 0.13 sec.
*****************************************/

#include <iostream>
#include <windows.h>
#include <math.h>

using namespace std;

const int MN = 1000;

typedef unsigned int UI;

UI x[305]; // max len = 302
int len; // number of digits

// x = x * (2^lshift)
void ShiftLeft(int lshift) {
```

```
    UI c = 0, d;
    for (int i = 0; i < len; ++i) {
     x[i] = (x[i] << lshift) + c;
     //x[i]=x[i]*(2^lsift)+c
     c = x[i] / 10;
     x[i] -= c*10;
     } // for
    while (c > 0) {
     d = c / 10;
     x[len++] = c - d*10;
     c = d;
     } // while
 } // ShiftLeft

int E16B(int lshift) {
  int i, sum;
  len = 1;
  x[0] = 1;
  int numloop = MN / lshift;
  for (i = 0; i < numloop; ++i) ShiftLeft(lshift);
  sum = 0;
  for (i = 0; i < len; ++i)   sum += x[i];
  return sum;
} // E16B

main() {
   cout << "\n Shift left 25 bits: " << E16B(25);
      // 2^25 = 3554432
   cout << "\n Shift left 1 bit: " << E16B(1);
   // 2^1 = 2
   cout << "\n  T H E    E N D .";
   return 0;
}
```

Free Pascal Program

```
(*****************************************
   Problem 16. Power digit sum
   Version E16B
   Answer = 1366, Time = 0.13 sec.
*****************************************)
const MN = 1000;
type int = integer;
var
```

```
  x: array[1..305] of longint;
  len: int;

// x = x * 2^(lshif);
procedure ShiftLeft(lshift: int);
  var  i: int;
  c, d: longint;
begin
  c := 0;
  for i := 1 to len do
  begin
    x[i] := (x[i] shl lshift) + c;
    c := x[i] div 10;
    x[i] := x[i] - c*10;
  end; // for
  while (c > 0) do
  begin
    d := c div 10;
    inc(len);
    x[len] := c - d*10;
    c := d;
  end; // while
end; // ShiftLeft

procedure E16B(lshift: int);
  var i, sum: int;
  numloop: int;
begin
  len := 1; x[1] := 1;
  numloop := MN div lshift;
  for i := 1 to numloop do ShiftLeft(lshift);
  sum := 0;
  for i := 1 to len do sum := sum + x[i];
  writeln(sum);
end; // E16B

BEGIN
  E16B(25); // 1366
  writeln('  T H E    E N D .');
  readln;
END.
```

Java Program

```
/***********************************
   Problem 16. Power digit sum
   Version E16C
   Answer = 1366, Time = 0.13 sec.
***********************************/
import java.math.*;

public class E16 {
  private static int MN = 1000;
  private int[] x = new int[305]; // maxlen = 302
  private int len = 0; // The length of x
  E16(){
    System.out.println("\n E16C: " + e16C(25));
  } // E16

  private int e16C(int lshift) {
    int sum = 0;
    len = 1; // The length of x
    int numloop = MN / lshift;
    x[0] = 1;
    for (int i = 0; i < numloop; ++i)
      ShiftLeft(lshift);
    for (int i = 0; i < len; ++i)
      sum += x[i];
    return sum;
  } // e16C

  // x = x * (2^lshift)
  private void ShiftLeft(int lshift) {
    int c = 0, d = 0;
    for (int i = 0; i < len; ++i) {
      x[i] = (x[i] << lshift) + c;
      c = x[i] / 10;
      x[i] -= c*10;
    } // for
    while (c > 0) {
      d = c / 10;
      x[len++] = c - d*10;
      c = d;
    } // while
  } // ShiftLeft
} // class E16
```

Problem 17. Number letter counts

If the numbers 1 to 5 are written out in words: one, two, three, four, five, then there are $3 + 3 + 5 + 4 + 4 = 19$ letters used in total.

If all the numbers from 1 to 1000 (one thousand) inclusive were written out in words, how many letters would be used?

NOTE: Do not count spaces or hyphens. For example, 342 (three hundred and forty-two) contains 23 letters and 115 (one hundred and fifteen) contains 20 letters. The use of "and" when writing out numbers is in compliance with British usage.

Understanding

When we are teaching a robot to speak, we need construct a similar software.

Algorithm

We'll try to design three variants:

E17A: Write out in words (WW) all the numbers from 1 to 1000.

E17B: WW a selected integer between 1 and 1000.

E17C: Calculate the number of the letters using to WW all the numbers from 1 to 1000.

Note that E17C is the answer for the Problem.

The first step is writing out in words the basic numbers, the conjunction "and" and the space " ". They are

- All the numbers from 1 to 19.
- All the numbers 20, 30, ..., 90
- 100
- 1000

Basic WW			
1	one		
2	two	20	twenty
3	three	30	thirty
4	four	40	forty
5	five	50	fifty
6	six	60	sixty
7	seven	70	seventy
8	eight	80	eighty
9	nine	90	ninety
10	ten	100	hundred
11	eleven	1000	thousand
12	twelve	BL	" "
13	thirteen	hyphen	" - "
14	fourteen	and	and
15	fifteen		
16	sixteen		
17	seventeen		
18	eighteen		
19	nineteen		

Let $WW(n)$ be the algorithm for writing in words a given natural number n, $1 \leq n \leq 1000$. We distinguish the following cases of parameter n.

- $n = 1000$ is the maximum number: $WW(1000) = $ "thousand".
- $100 \leq n \leq 999$: $WW(n) = WW(h) + BL + $ "hundred" + (if $m \neq 0$ then $BL + $ "and" + $WW(m)$ endif),

  where $h = n$ div 100, $m = n$ mod 100, BL is space symbol.
- $n < 20$: $WW(n)$.

- $20 \leq n \leq 99$: $WW(n) = WW(n - v) + ($if $v \neq 0$ then hyphen $+ WW(v)$ endif$)$, where $v = n \bmod 10$.

Replacing WW operator by get length we can count the length for each number and its total length.

C++ Program

```
/*********************************************
  Problem 17. Number letter counts
  Answer = 21124 (E17C, Time = 0.08 sec.)
*********************************************/
#include <iostream>
#include <windows.h>

using namespace std;

const string w19[20] =
  {"","one","two","three","four","five",
  "six","seven", "eight","nine","ten",
  "eleven","twelve","thirteen", "fourteen",
  "fifteen","sixteen","seventeen",
  "eighteen", "nineteen"}; // 1-19

const string wx0[10] =
  {"","","twenty","thirty","forty","fifty",
  "sixty","seventy","eighty","ninety"}; //10-90
  // Note: forty (correct), but fourty (incorect)
const string whundred = "hundred";
const string wand = "and";
const string BL = " ";
const string hyphen = "-";
const string wthousand = "thousand";

bool Stop() {
  fflush(stdin);
  cout << "\n Press dot key (.) to stop "
     << " or another key to continue: ";
  return (cin.get() == '.');
} // Stop

void WW(int n) {
  if (n < 1 || n > 1000) return;
  if (n == 1000) {
```

```
      cout << w19[1] << BL << wthousand;
      return;
  } // if n == 1000
  // 1 <= n < 1000
    if (n > 99) { // 100 <= (n = abc) < 1000
      cout << w19[n / 100] << BL << whundred; // a
      n %= 100; // n = bc
      if (n == 0) return;
      cout << BL << wand;
    } // if n > 99
    if (n < 20) { // (n = bc) < 20
      cout << BL << w19[n];
      return;
    } // if n < 20
    // 20 <= (n = bc) <= 99
    cout << BL << wx0[n / 10];
    n %= 10;
    if (n == 0) return;
    cout << hyphen << w19[n % 10];
} // WW

//  Write out in words all the numbers from 1 to 1000.
void E17A() {
  int n;
  cout << "\n\n E17A.\n";
  for (n = 1; n <= 1000; ++n) {
    cout << "\n  " << n << ": "; WW(n);
    if (n % 20 == 0) {
      if (Stop()) return;
    } // if
  } // for
} // E17A

// Write out in words a selected integer
// in the range [1; 1000].
void E17B() {
  int n;
  cout << "\n\n E17B.\n";
  while (1) {
    fflush(stdin);
    cout << "\n Get a number between 1..1000: ";
    cout << "\n To stop, get n < 1 or n > 1000: ";
    cin >> n;
    if (n < 1 || n > 1000) return;
```

```cpp
    cout << "    *** " << n << ": ";
    WW(n); cout << ".";
  } // while
} // E17B

// Get the length of WW(n)
  int Count(int n) {
   int c = 0;
   if (n < 1 || n > 1000) return c;
   if (n == 1000) {
     return w19[1].length() + wthousand.length();
   } // if n == 1000
   // 1 <= n < 1000
   if (n > 99) { // 100 <= (n = abc) < 1000
     c += w19[n / 100].length() +
         whundred.length();//a
    n %= 100; // n = bc
    if (n == 0) return c;
    c += wand.length();
   } // if n > 99
   if (n < 20) { // (n = bc) < 20
     return c + w19[n].length();
   } // if n < 20
   // 20 <= (n = bc) <= 99
   return c + wx0[n / 10].length()
      + w19[n % 10].length();
   } // Count

  void E17C() {
   int n, sum = 0;
   for (n = 1; n <= 1000; ++n) sum += Count(n);
   cout << "\n\n E17C. Total: " << sum << ".";
   if (Stop()) exit(0);
   } // E17C

  main() {
    E17C(); // 21124
    E17A();
    E17B();
    cout << "\n  T H E    E N D .";
    return 0;
  }
```

Free Pascal Program

```
(*********************************************
   Problem 17. Number letter counts
   Answer = 21124 (E17C, Time = 0.08 sec.)
*********************************************)
  uses crt;
  type int = integer;
  const BL = #32; NL = #13#10; ESC = #27;
     hyphen = '-';
  whundred = 'hundred';
  wand = 'and';
  wthousand = 'thousand';
// Note: forty (correct), but fourty (incorect)
w19: array[0..19] of string[9] =
('','one','two','three','four','five',
'six','seven', 'eight','nine','ten',
'eleven','twelve','thirteen', 'fourteen','fifteen',
'sixteen','seventeen','eighteen', 'nineteen'); //0-19
wx0: array[0..9] of string[7] =
('','','twenty','thirty','forty',
'fifty','sixty','seventy','eighty','ninety'); //10-90

function Stop: Boolean;
  var ch: char;
begin
  write(NL,' Press dot key (.) to stop');
  write(' or another key to continue: ');
  ch := ReadKey;
  writeln;
  Stop := (ch = '.');
end;

procedure WW(n: int);
begin
  if (n < 1) or (n > 1000) then exit;
  if (n = 1000) then
  begin
    writeln(w19[1], BL, wthousand);
    exit;
  end; // if
  // 1 <= n < 1000
  if (n > 99) then
  begin // 100 <= (n = abc) < 1000
```

```
    write(w19[n div 100], BL, whundred); // a
    n := n mod 100; // n = bc
    if (n = 0) then exit;
    write(BL, wand);
  end; // if
  if (n < 20) then
  begin // (n = bc) < 20
    writeln(BL, w19[n]);
    exit;
  end; // if
  // 20 <= (n = bc) <= 99
  write(BL, wx0[n div 10]);
  n := n mod 10;
  if (n = 0) then
  begin
    writeln;
    exit;
  end;
    writeln(hyphen, w19[n]);
end;

// write in words all the numbers
// from 1 to 1000
procedure E17A;
  var n: int;
begin
  writeln('  E17A.');
  for n := 1 to 1000 do
  begin
    write('    ', n, ': '); WW(n); // write('.');
    if (n mod 20 = 0) then
      if Stop then exit;
  end; // for
end; // E17A

// Write in words a selected number
// in the range [1; 1000]
procedure E17B;
  var n: int;
begin
  writeln('  E17B. ');
  while (true) do
  begin
    write(NL,' Get a number between 1..1000. ');
```

```
    write(NL,' To stop get n < 1 or n > 1000: ');
    readln(n);
    writeln;
    if (n < 1) or (n > 1000) then exit;
    write(' ***    ', n, ': '); WW(n);
  end; // while
end; // E17B

// The length of WW(n)
function Count(n: int): int;
  var c: int;
begin
  c := 0;
  if (n < 1) or (n > 1000) then exit(c);
  if (n = 1000) then
  begin
    exit(length(w19[1]) + length(wthousand));
  end; // if

  // 1 <= n < 1000
  if (n > 99) then
  begin // 100 <= (n = abc) < 1000
    c := c+length(w19[n div 100])+length(whundred);//a
    n := n mod 100; // n = bc
    if (n = 0) then exit(c);
    c := c + length(wand);
  end; // if

  if (n < 20) then
  begin // (n = bc) < 20
    exit(c + length(w19[n]));
  end;
  // 20 <= (n = bc) <= 99
  exit (c + length(wx0[n div 10])
      + length(w19[n mod 10]));
end; // Count

procedure E17C;
  var n, sum: int;
begin
  sum := 0;
  for n := 1 to 1000 do
    sum := sum + Count(n);
  writeln(NL,' E17C.  Total: ', sum);
```

```
  if Stop then halt;
end; // E17C

BEGIN
  E17C; // 21124
  E17A;
  E17B;
  writeln('   T H E    E N D .');
  readln;
END.
```

Java Program

```
/*******************************************
   Problem 17. Number letter counts
   Answer = 21124 (E17C, Time = 0.08 sec.)
*******************************************/
import java.io.*; // IOException;

public class E17 {
private String w19[] = {
   "","one","two","three","four","five",
   "six","seven", "eight","nine","ten",
   "eleven","twelve","thirteen", "fourteen",
   "fifteen","sixteen","seventeen",
   "eighteen", "nineteen" }; //1-19

private String wx0[] = {
   "","","twenty","thirty","forty","fifty",
   "sixty","seventy","eighty","ninety"};
// 10-90
// Note: forty (correct)
   private String whundred = "hundred";
   private String wand = "and";
   private String BL = " ";
   private String hyphen = "-";
   private String wthousand = "thousand";

  E17(){
    e17C(); // 21124
    if (Stop()) System.exit(0);
    e17B();
    e17A();
    System.out.println("\n Bye!");
```

```
}

 private Boolean Stop() {
  int c = 0;
  System.out.print("\n Press dot key [.] to stop\n"+
        " or other key to continue: ");
  try {
    c = System.in.read();
  }
  catch (IOException e){
    System.out.println();
  }
  return (c == '.');
 } // Stop

 // Sum of letters using to write all numbers
 // from 1 to 1000
 public void e17C() {
  int n = 0, sum = 0;
  for (n = 1; n <= 1000; ++n)
    sum += count(n);
  System.out.println("\n e17C. Total: " + sum);
 } // e17C

 // length of WW(n)
 private int count(int n) {
  int c = 0;
  if (n < 1 || n > 1000) return c;
  if (n == 1000) {
    return w19[1].length()+wthousand.length();
  } // if n == 1000
  // 1 <= n < 1000
  if (n > 99) { // 100 <= (n = abc) < 1000
    c += w19[n / 100].length() + whundred.length();
  // a
    n %= 100; // n = bc
    if (n == 0) return c;
    c += wand.length();
  } // if n > 99
  if (n < 20) { // (n = bc) < 20
    return c + w19[n].length();
  } // if n < 20
  // 20 <= (n = bc) <= 99
  return c + wx0[n / 10].length()
```

```
    + w19[n % 10].length();
} // Count

private void WW(int n) {
 if (n < 1 || n > 1000) return;
 if (n == 1000) {
   System.out.print(w19[1]+ " " + wthousand);
   return;
 } // if n == 1000
 // 1 <= n < 1000
 if (n > 99) { // 100 <= (n = abc) < 1000
 System.out.print( w19[n/100]+" "+whundred); // a
   n %= 100; // n = bc
   if (n == 0) return;
   System.out.print(" " + wand);
 } // if n > 99
 if (n < 20) { // (n = bc) < 20
   System.out.print(" "+w19[n]);
   return;
 } // if n < 20
 // 20 <= (n = bc) <= 99
 System.out.print(" " + wx0[n/10]);
 n %= 10;
 if (n == 0) return;
 System.out.print(hyphen + w19[n]);
} // WW

// Write in words of all numbers
// from 1 to 1000
private void e17A() {
 int n;
 for (n = 1; n <= 1000; ++n) {
   System.out.print("\n  " + n + ": "); WW(n);
   if (n % 20 == 0) {
   if (Stop()) return;
   }
 } // for
} // e17A
// Write in words a selected number
// in range [1; 1000]
private void e17B() {
 int n = 0;
 while (true) {
   System.out.print("\n Get a number n ");
```

```
    System.out.print(" between 1...1000. ");
    System.out.print("\n To stop, get n < 1");
    System.out.print(" or n > 1000: ");
    try {
    BufferedReader in =
    new BufferedReader(new
    InputStreamReader(System.in));
    n = Integer.parseInt(in.readLine());
    }
    catch (IOException e){
    System.out.print("\n Err.");
    }
    if (n < 1 || n > 1000) return;
    System.out.print("\n " + n + ": ");
    WW(n);
  } // while
  } // e17B
} // class e17
```

Problem 18. Maximum sum in the triangle

By starting at the top of the triangle below and moving to adjacent numbers on the row below, the maximum total from top to bottom is 23.

$$
\begin{array}{c}
3 \\
7 \quad 4 \\
2 \quad 4 \quad 6 \\
8 \quad 5 \quad 9 \quad 3
\end{array}
$$

That is, $3 + 7 + 4 + 9 = 23$.

Find the maximum total from top to bottom of the triangle below:

```
                        75
                      95 64
                    17 47 82
                  18 35 87 10
                20 04 82 47 65
              19 01 23 75 03 34
            88 02 77 73 07 63 67
          99 65 04 28 06 16 70 92
        41 41 26 56 83 40 80 70 33
      41 48 72 33 47 32 37 16 94 29
    53 71 44 65 25 43 91 52 97 51 14
  70 11 33 28 77 73 17 78 39 68 17 57
91 71 52 38 17 14 91 43 58 50 27 29 48
63 66 04 68 89 53 67 30 73 16 69 87 40 31
04 62 98 27 23 09 70 98 73 93 38 53 60 04 23
```

NOTE: As there are only 16384 routes, it is possible to solve this problem by trying every route. However, Problem 67, is the same challenge with a triangle containing one-hundred rows; it cannot be solved by brute force, and requires a clever method!)

Understanding

This problem is included in the 6th International Olympiad in Informatics (IOI), Sweden, 1994.

Algorithm

The problem can be solved by the *dynamic programming method.*

First, we need to know that the indexes of each line are numbered from 1. The line r^{th} has r numbers, indexing from 1 to r. For example,

Index	1	2	3	4	5	6	7
row 1	75						
row 2	95	64					
...							
row 6	19	1	23	75	3	34	
row 7	88	2	77	73	7	63	67

From position k in row r we can only move to the two positions k or $k+1$ of the next row $r+1$ below. For example, from number **23** in row 6 we can move to numbers **77** or **73** of row 7. Conversely, the number 67 in row 7 is the "arrival number" of number 34 in row 6.

Suppose that the triangle has n rows. Denote by

A the top point of the triangle,

$r(k)$ the value of the kth number in row r,

$v(r, k)$ the maximum "income" value, getting after moving from A to position k of the row r.

Examples

$6(3) = 23$.

$v(1, 1) = 75$.

$v(2,1) = 75 + 95 = 170$.

$v(2,2) = 75 + 64 = 139$.

To move optimally from A to position k of row r, first we need to go to one of the two preceding positions $k-1$ or k in row $r-1$ above r and then add one step to the k. This means that

$$v(r, k) = \max \{v(r-1, k-1) + r(k), \ v(r-1, k) + r(k)\}, \text{ or }$$

$$v(r,\ k) = \max \{v(r{-}1,\ k{-}1),\ v(r{-}1,\ k)\} + r(k) \qquad (18.1)$$

$$1 \le r \le 15,\ 1 \le k \le r.$$

we accept $v(r,\ 0) = 0$, and $v(0,\ k) = 0$.

(18.1) is called the *dynamic programming formula* (or *Bellman equation*). This formula usually is a recursive function, hence some values $v(r,\ k)$ can be calculated repeatedly with many times. We will organize a such algorithm that each $v(r,\ k)$, $1 \le r \le n$, $1 \le k \le r$ is calling no more one time. To do this, we use an array val[] to save the values $v(r,\ k)$. When we scan row r from position r backward to 1, we compute val[k] = $v(r,\ k)$.

Algorithm E18

Input: n rows of given triangle.
Output: max v(n, k), $1 \le k \le n$.
begin
    for r ← 1 to n do // scan row r
        for k ← r down to 1 // scan each position k in r
          val[k] ←v(r, k); // save v(r,k)
        endfor k
    endfor r
    return max {val[1], val[2], ..., val[n]};
endE18

Suppose the input data is written in the one-dimensional array nums[], where nums[0] = 0 is not used. We know that r^{th} row has r numbers. These numbers are saved in the array nums[] as follow,

    row 1: nums[1],

    row 2: nums[2], nums[3],

    row 3: nums[4], nums[5], nums[6],

    row 4: nums[7], nums[8], nums[9], nums[10],

    ...

For each position k from 1 to r of row r, we need to point out the absolute index of k in the array nums[]. The first absolute index of row r is

$$d(r) = 1 + 2 + \cdots + (r-1) + 1 = \frac{r(r-1)}{2} + 1 \qquad (Gauss)$$

The last absolute index of row r is

$$c(r) = d(r) + r - 1$$

For example, in row 7, we have $d(7) = 22$, $c(7) = 28$ and the input values are

$7(1) = \text{nums}[22] = 88,$

$7(2) = \text{nums}[23] = 2,$

$7(3) = \text{nums}[24] = 77,$

$7(4) = \text{nums}[25] = 73,$

$7(5) = \text{nums}[26] = 7,$

$7(6) = \text{nums}[27] = 63,$ and

$7(7) = \text{nums}[28] = 67.$

It is better if we use the following recursive relations to set the first $d(r)$ and the last $c(r)$ absolute indexes of row r.

$d(r) = c(r-1) + 1,$

$c(r) = c(r-1) + r,$

with $c(0) = 0$.

C++ Program

```
/*************************************************
   Problem 18. Maximum sum in the triangle
   Answer = 1074, Time = 0.12 sec.
*************************************************/

#include <iostream>
#include <windows.h>

using namespace std;

const int MN = 15; // 15 rows
```

```
int nums[] = {0,
   75,
   95,64,
   17,47,82,
   18,35,87,10,
   20,4, 82,47,65,
   19, 1,23,75,3,34,
   88, 2, 77,73,7,63,67,
   99,65, 4,28, 6,16,70,92,
   41,41,26,56,83,40,80,70,33,
   41,48,72,33,47,32,37,16,94,29,
   53,71,44,65,25,43,91,52,97,51,14,
   70,11,33,28,77,73,17,78,39,68,17,57,
   91,71,52,38,17,14,91,43,58,50,27,29,48,
   63,66,4, 68,89,53,67,30,73,16,69,87,40,31,
   4,62,98,27,23, 9,70,98,73,93,38,53,60, 4,23};

int val[MN+1]; // to save v(r, k)


void E18() {
  int maxval, c = 0, i, k;
  // Dynamic programming
  memset(val, 0, sizeof(val));
  for(int r = 1; r <= MN; ++r) { // Scan each row r
    c += r;//absolute index of the last number in row r
    // backward process row r
    for(i = r, k = c; i > 0; --k, --i) {
      val[i] = max(val[i], val[i-1]) + nums[k];
    } // for i
  } // for r
  // Get maxval from val[1...n];
  maxval = val[1];
  for (i = 2; i <= MN; ++i)
    if (maxval < val[i]) maxval = val[i];
  cout << "\n Result: " << maxval;
}// E18

main() {
  E18(); // 1074
  cout << "\n  T H E    E N D .";
  return 0;
}
```

Free Pascal Program

```
(* * * * * * * * * * * * * * * * * * * * * * * * * * * * * * * * * * * * * * * * * * * * *
   Problem 18. Maximum sum in the triangle
   Answer =  1074, Time = 0.12 sec.
* * * * * * * * * * * * * * * * * * * * * * * * * * * * * * * * * * * * * * * * * * *)
const MN = 15;
MN2 = (1+MN)*MN div 2;
type int = integer;
const
nums: array[0..MN2] of int = ( 0,
  75,
  95,64,
  17,47,82,
  18,35,87,10,
  20,4, 82,47,65,
  19, 1,23,75,3,34,
  88, 2, 77,73,7,63,67,
  99,65, 4,28, 6,16,70,92,
  41,41,26,56,83,40,80,70,33,
  41,48,72,33,47,32,37,16,94,29,
  53,71,44,65,25,43,91,52,97,51,14,
  70,11,33,28,77,73,17,78,39,68,17,57,
  91,71,52,38,17,14,91,43,58,50,27,29,48,
  63,66,4, 68,89,53,67,30,73,16,69,87,40,31,
  4,62,98,27,23, 9,70,98,73,93,38,53,60, 4,23);
var
  val: array[0..MN+1] of int;// to save v(r, k)

procedure  E18;
  var i, k, r, maxval: int;
  c: int;
begin
  // Dynamic programming
  fillchar(val, sizeof(val), 0);
  c := 0;
  for r := 1 to MN do
  begin
    c:=c+r; //absolute index of last number in row r
    // scan row r
    k := c;
    for i := r downto 1 do
    begin
      if val[i-1] > val[i] then val[i] := val[i-1];
```

```
    val[i] := val[i] + nums[k];
    dec(k);
  end; // for i
 end; // for r
 maxval := val[1];
 // Get maxval
 for i := 2 to MN do
   if (val[i] > maxval) then maxval := val[i];
 writeln(' Result: ', maxval);
end; // E18

BEGIN
  E18; // 1074
  writeln('  T H E    E N D .');
  readln;
END.
```

Java Program

```
/********************************************
   Problem 18. Maximum sum in the triangle
   Answer = 1074, Time = 0.12 sec.
********************************************/
import java.util.Arrays;

public class E18 {
  private int[] nums = {0,
    75,
    95,64,
    17,47,82,
    18,35,87,10,
    20, 4,82,47,65,
    19, 1,23,75, 3,34,
    88, 2,77,73, 7,63,67,
    99,65, 4,28, 6,16,70,92,
    41,41,26,56,83,40,80,70,33,
    41,48,72,33,47,32,37,16,94,29,
    53,71,44,65,25,43,91,52,97,51,14,
    70,11,33,28,77,73,17,78,39,68,17,57,
    91,71,52,38,17,14,91,43,58,50,27,29,48,
    63,66, 4,68,89,53,67,30,73,16,69,87,40,31,
     4,62,98,27,23, 9,70,98,73,93,38,53,60, 4,23};
  private int n = 15;
  private int[] val = new int[n+3];
```

```java
  private int end = 0;

  E18() {
   // Dynamic programming
   Arrays.fill(val,0);
   for(int r = 1; r <= n; ++r) {
     // set start and end indexes for the row r
     end += r;
     // process row r
     for(int i = r, k = end; i > 0; --k, --i) {
     val[i] = Math.max(val[i], val[i-1]) + nums[k];
     } // for i
   } // for r
   // Get maxval in val[1..row];
   int maxval = val[1];
   for (int i = 2; i <= n; ++i)
     if (maxval < val[i]) maxval = val[i];
   System.out.println("\n Result: " + maxval);//1074
  } // E18
} // class E18
```

Problem 19. How many Sundays on the first of a month ?

You are given the following information, but you may prefer to do some research for yourself.

1 Jan 1900 was a Monday.

Thirty days has September,

April, June and November.

All the rest have thirty-one,

Saving February alone,

Which has twenty-eight, rain or shine.

And on leap years, twenty-nine.

A leap year occurs on any year evenly divisible by 4, but not on a century unless it is divisible by 400.

How many Sundays fell on the first of the month during the twentieth century (1 Jan 1901 to 31 Dec 2000)?

Understanding

The given information is shown in the following table.

Month	Jan	Feb	Mar	Apr	May	Jun	Jul	Aug	Sep	Oct	Nov	Dec
	1	2	3	4	5	6	7	8	9	10	11	12
Number of days	31	28/29	31	30	31	30	31	31	30	31	30	31

Feb. has 29 days in the *leap year*, and 28 days in the *common year*.

Year *abcd* is a leap year if: ($cd \neq 00$ and cd mod 4 = 0)

or ($cd = 00$ and ab mod 4 = 0)

The next algorithm checks if a given year is a leap year.

```
Algorithm LeapYear
Input:  year
Output: True if year is a leap year; false otherwise.
begin
    // year has the form abcd (ab × 100 + cd)
    // for example 2018 gives ab = 20, cd = 18
    ab ← year div 100;
    cd ← year mod 100;
    if (cd = 0) then return ((ab mod 4) = 0);
        else return ((cd mod 4) = 0) endif;
endLeapYear
```

Algorithm

We follow the formulas of the outstanding German mathematician Carl Friedrich Gauss. These formulas have appeared in his manuscript.

The weekday codes

Gauss gives Sunday the code 0, Monday: 1, …

Day	Sun	Mon	Tue	Wed	Thu	Fri	Sat
Code	0	1	2	3	4	5	6

The first weekday of a year

To find code w of the first weekday of year y (January 1st y), we use the formula

$$w = (A + B + C + 1) \bmod 7 \qquad (19.1)$$

where

$A = 5((y-1) \bmod 4)$

$B = 4((y-1) \bmod 100)$

$C = 6((y-1) \bmod 400)$

```
Algorithm FirstWeekday

Input:  year y
Output: weekday code of 1st Jan y
begin
    y ← y - 1;
    return (5*(y mod 4) + 4*(y mod 100) + 6*(y mod 400) + 1) mod 7;
endFirstWeekday.
```

Examples

1. Find weekday of 1st January 2018.

We have

$y - 1 = 2018 - 1 = 2017.$

$A = 5(2017 \bmod 4) = 5(17 \bmod 4) = 5 \times 1 = 5.$

$B = 4(2017 \bmod 100) = 4 \times 17 = 68.$

$C = 6(2017 \bmod 400) = 6((2000 \bmod 400) + 17) = 6 \times 17 = 102.$

Hence, $w = (A + B + C + 1) \bmod 7 = (5 + 68 + 102 + 1) \bmod 7 = 1.$

Therefore, 1st Jan. 2018 is *Monday* (code 1).

2. Find weekday of 1st January 1900.

We have,

$y - 1 = 1900 - 1 = 1899.$

$A = 5(1899 \bmod 4) = 5(99 \bmod 4) = 5 \times 3 = 15.$

$B = 4(1899 \bmod 100) = 4 \times 99 = 396.$

$C = 6(1899 \bmod 400) = 6(1800 \bmod 400) + 99) = 6 \times 299 = 1794.$

$w = (A + B + C + 1) \bmod 7 = (15 + 396 + 1794 + 1) \bmod 7 = (1 + 4 + 2 + 1) \bmod 7 = 1.$

Therefore, 1st Jan. 1900 is *Monday* (code 1).

The weekday of day d-m-y

To find code w of the weekday of day d, month m, year y, we use the formula

$$w = (w' + C + d - 1) \bmod 7 \qquad\qquad (19.2)$$

where,

w' is the first weekday of year y,

C is the coefficient of month m (see Tab. 19.1)

d is the given day.

Month coefficients of the leap year and common (or ordinary) year are different.

Code	Month	Com. year	Leap year
1	January	0	0
2	February	3	3
3	March	3	4
4	April	6	0
5	May	1	2
6	June	4	5
7	July	6	0
8	August	2	3
9	September	5	6
10	October	0	1
11	November	3	4
12	December	5	6

Tab. 19.1. Coefficients of the months

We use a two-dimensional array MONT_COEFF[t][m] to represent the coefficients of month m, where t = 1 (true) for the leap year, and t = 0 (false) for the common year. For example,

June 2018 has coefficient MONTH_COEFF[0][6] = 4,

June 2016 has coefficient MONTH_COEFF[1][6] = 5.

Therefore, MONTH_COEFF[LeapYear(y)][m] give the coefficient of month m, year y.

Algorithm Weekday

Input: day, month, year
Output: weekday code of day-month-year
begin
   return (FirstWeekday(year)
       + Month_Coeff[LeapYear(year)][month]
       + day - 1) mod 7;
endWeekday.

Examples

1. Find the weekday of 1st May 2018.

We have

$w' = 1$ (previous example, 1st Jan 2018.)

$C = 1$ (Tab. 19.1, May)

$d = 1$

$w = (w' + C + d - 1) \bmod 7 = (1 + 1 + 1 - 1) \bmod 7 = 2$.

Therefore, 1st May 2018 is *Tuesday* (code 2).

2. Find the weekday of 5 June 2020.

First, we find the first weekday of 2020. We have,

$y - 1 = 2020 - 1 = 2019$.

$A = 5(2019 \bmod 4) = 5(19 \bmod 4) = 5 \times 3 = 15$.

$B = 4(2019 \bmod 100) = 4 \times 19 = 76$.

$C = 6(2019 \bmod 400) = 6((2000 \bmod 400) + 19) = 6 \times 19 = 114$

$w = (A + B + C + 1) \bmod 7 = (15 + 76 + 114 + 1) \bmod 7 = (1 + 6 + 2 + 1) \bmod 7 = 3$.

Therefore, the first weekday of 2020 is *Wednesday* (code 3).

Now we calculate the weekday of 5-6-2020.

2020 is a leap year.

$w' = 3$.

$C = 5$ (Tab. 19.1, Jun. of leap year)

$d = 5$.

$w = (w' + C + d - 1) \bmod 7 = (3 + 5 + 5 - 1) \bmod 7 = 5$.

Therefore, 5 June 2020 is *Friday* (code 5).

First, we give two versions E19A and E19B for the Problem 19.

E19A

Scan all years of the XX Century, from 1901 to 2000 and calculate how many Sundays fell on the first of the month of each year. Function Weekday(1, m, y) returns the weekday code (0: Sunday, 1: Monday, ..., 6: Saturday) of the first of month m, year y (1st-m-y) . So, clause

```
if (Weekday(1, m, y) = 0)
```

returns the value true if 1st-m-y is Sunday (has the weekday code 0).

```
Algorithm E19A
Input: years 1901 – 2000 (XX Century)
Output: Number of Sundays of 1st-m, 1 ≤ m ≤ 12.
begin
    count ← 0;
    for year ← 1901 to 2000 do
        for month ← 1 to 12 do
            if (Weekday(1, month, year) = 0)  then
            // 0 is Sunday
                count ← count + 1;
            endif
        endfor month
    endfor year
    return  count;
endE19A
```

E19B

We follow the formula of weekday of d-m-y

$$w = (w' + C + d - 1) \bmod 7.$$

Since we need to find the weekday on the first day of month ($d = 1$), we get the following formula,

$w1 = (w' + C + d - 1) \bmod 7 = (w' + C + 1 - 1) \bmod 7 = (w' + C) \bmod 7.$

where w' is the first weekday of the year, C is the coefficient of month m. To get Sunday (code 0) on the first of month, we set the following relation,

$$(w' + C) \bmod 7 = 0 \qquad (19.3)$$

In the other word, the sum $(w' + C)$ is a multiple of 7, for example $w' + C = 0, 7, 14, \ldots$

But, we know that $0 \le w'$, $C \le 6$, it follows that $0 \le w' + C \le 12$. So, testing $(w' + C) \bmod 7 = 0$ is equivalent to $(w' + C) = 0$ or $(w' + C) = 7$, and we will use the last relation, because the operation mod is complicated.

```
Algorithm E19B
Input: years 1901 – 2000 (XX Century)
Output: Number of Sundays of 1st-m, 1 ≤ m ≤ 12.
begin
    count ← 0;
    for year ← 1901 to 2000 do
        leap ← LeapYear(year);
        w' ← FirstWeekday(year);
        for month ← 1 to 12 do
            v ← w' + Month_Coeff[leap][month] ;
            if (v = 0) or (v = 7) then  count ← count+1 endif;
        endfor month
    endfor year
    return count;
endE19B
```

C++ Program

```
/**********************************************
   Problem 19.  How many Sundays on the first
                of a month ?
   Answer = 171, Time = 0.07 sec.
   - Two variants E19A and E19B
**********************************************/
#include <iostream>
#include <windows.h>

using namespace std;

/*-------------------------------------------------
   Some leap years (February has 29 days)
   1904, 1908, 1912, 1916, 1920, 1924, 1928, 1932,
   1936, 1940,1944, 1948, 1952, 1956, 1960, 1964,
   1968, 1972, 1976, 1980,1984, 1988, 1992, 1996,
   2000, 2004, 2008, 2012, 2016, 2020.
-------------------------------------------------*/

int NUM_DAY_OF_MONTH[2][13] =
{{0,31,28,31,30,31,30,31,31,30,31,30,31},//com. year
{0,31,29,31,30,31,30,31,31,30,31,30,31}};//leap year

int MONTH_COEFF[2][13] =
{{0,0,3,3,6,1,4,6,2,5,0,3,5}, // common year
{0,0,3,4,0,2,5,0,3,6,1,4,6}}; // leap year

bool LeapYear(int year) {
  // year = abcd
  int ab = year / 100;
  int cd = year - 100*ab;
  return (cd == 0)? ((ab % 4)== 0): ((cd % 4)==0);
} // LeapYear

// The first weekday of the year (Gauss)
// Sunday = 0, ..., Saturday = 6
int FirstWeekday(int year) {
  --year;
  return (1+5*(year%4)+4*(year%100)+6*(year%400))%7;
}// FirstWeekday

// Week day
```

```
int WeekDay(int day, int month, int year) {
  return (FirstWeekday(year)
    + MONTH_COEFF[LeapYear(year)][month]+day-1)%7;
} // WeekDay

// Number of Sundays on 1 - month in XX Century
void E19A() {
  int count = 0;
  int year, month;
  for (year = 1901; year <= 2000; ++year) {
    for (month = 1; month <= 12; ++month)
      if (WeekDay(1,month,year) == 0)
      ++count;
  } // for year
  cout << "\n E19A Result:  " << count;
} // E19A

// Number of Sundays on 1st - month in year
int NumOfSun(int year) {
  int weekday, month;
  int count = 0;
  int v;
  bool leap = LeapYear(year);
  weekday = FirstWeekday(year);
  for (month = 1; month <= 12; ++month){
    v = weekday + MONTH_COEFF[leap][month];
    if (v == 0 || v == 7) ++count;
  } // for
  return count;
}

// Number of Sundays on 1 - month in XX Century
void E19B() {
  int sum = 0;
  for (int year = 1901; year <= 2000; ++year)
    sum += NumOfSun(year);
  cout << "\n E19B Result:  " << sum;
} // E19B
main() {
  E19A(); // 171
  E19B(); // 171
  cout << "\n T H E    E N D .";
  return 0;
}
```

Pascal Program

```
(* * * * * * * * * * * * * * * * * * * * * * * * * * * * * * * * * * * * * * * * * * * * * * * * * *
   Problem 19.   How many Sundays on the first
             of a month ?
   Answer = 171, Time = 0.07 sec.
   - Two variant E19A, E19B
* * * * * * * * * * * * * * * * * * * * * * * * * * * * * * * * * * * * * * * * * * * * * * * * * *)

(*-------------------------------------------------
   Some leap years (February has 29 days)
   1904, 1908, 1912, 1916, 1920, 1924, 1928, 1932,
   1936, 1940,1944, 1948, 1952, 1956, 1960, 1964,
   1968, 1972, 1976, 1980,1984, 1988, 1992, 1996,
   2000, 2004, 2008, 2012, 2016, 2020.
-------------------------------------------------*)

const NL = #13#10; BL = #32;
COMM = 0; LEAP = 1;
type int = integer;
MFORM = array[COMM..LEAP,1..12] of int;

const

NUM_DAY_OF_MONTH: MFORM =
((31,28,31,30,31,30,31,31,30,31,30,31),//common year
(31,29,31,30,31,30,31,31,30,31,30,31));//leap year

MONTH_COEFF: MFORM
= ((0,3,3,6,1,4,6,2,5,0,3,5),// common year
(0,3,4,0,2,5,0,3,6,1,4,6) ); // leap year

function LeapYear(year: int): byte;
  var ab, cd: int;
begin
  // year = ab|cd
  ab := year div  100;
  cd := year mod 100;
  if cd = 0 then
  begin
    if ab mod 4 = 0 then exit(1)
      else exit(0);
  end;
  if cd mod 4 = 0 then exit(1)
```

```
  else exit(0);
end; // LeapYear

// The first weekday of the year
function FirstWeekday(year: int): int;
begin
 dec(year);
 exit((1+5*(year mod 4)+4*(year mod 100)
      + 6*(year mod 400)) mod 7);
   end; // FirstWeekday

   // weekday of the day d-m-y
   function WeekDay(day, month, year: int): int;
   begin
     exit((FirstWeekday(year)
     + MONTH_COEFF[LeapYear(year),month]+day-1) mod 7);
   end; // WeekDay

   // Number of Sundays on 1 - month in XX Century
   procedure E19A;
     var count, month, year: int;
   begin
     count := 0;
     for year := 1901 to 2000 do
       for month := 1 to 12 do
         if WeekDay(1,month,year) = 0 then inc(count);
     writeln(NL, ' E19A Result:  ', count);
   end; // E19A

   // Number of Sundays on 1st-m in the year
   function NumOfSun(year: int): int;
    var weekday, count, month: int;
    leap: byte;
    v: int;
   begin
    leap := LeapYear(year);
    weekday := FirstWeekday(year);
    count := 0;
    for month := 1 to 12 do
    begin
      v := weekday + MONTH_COEFF[leap][month];
      if ((v = 0) or (v = 7)) then inc(count);
    end;
    exit(count);
```

```
    end; // NumOfSun

    // Number of Sundays on 1 - month in XX Century
    procedure E19B;
        var count, year: int;
    begin
        count := 0;
     for year := 1901 to 2000 do
     inc(count, NumOfSun(year));
   writeln(NL, ' E19B Result:  ', count);
end; // E19B

BEGIN
   E19A; // 171
   E19B; // 171
   writeln(NL, '  T H E    E N D .');
   readln;
END.
```

Java Program

```
/*********************************************
  Problem 19. How many Sundays on the first
          of a month ?
  Answer = 171, Time = 0.07 sec.
  Variants e19A, e19B
   Some leap years (February has 29 days)
   1904, 1908, 1912, 1916, 1920, 1924, 1928, 1932,
   1936, 1940,1944, 1948, 1952, 1956, 1960, 1964,
   1968, 1972, 1976, 1980,1984, 1988, 1992, 1996,
  2000, 2004, 2008, 2012, 2016, 2020.
*********************************************/
import java.io.*;

public class E19 {
private int[][] NUM_DAY_OF_MONTH =
{{0,31,28,31,30,31,30,31,31,30,31,30,31},//common year
{0,31,29,31,30,31,30,31,31,30,31,30,31}};//leap year
private int[][] MONTH_COEFF =
{{0,0,3,3,6,1,4,6,2,5,0,3,5}, // common year
{0,0,3,4,0,2,5,0,3,6,1,4,6}}; // leap year

private int SUNDAY = 0;
   E19(){
```

```
    e19A();
    e19B();
}

// 1 : leap year, 0: common year
private int leapYear(int year) {
  // year = abcd
  int ab = year / 100;
  int cd = year - 100*ab;
  if (cd == 0) {
    return ((ab % 4) == 0) ? 1 : 0;
  }
  return ((cd % 4) == 0) ? 1 : 0;
} // LeapYear

// The first weekday of the year (Gauss)
// Which weekday is 1/Jan/year ?
private int FirstWeekday(int year) {
  --year;
  return (1+5*(year%4)+4*(year%100)+6*(year%400))%7;
} // FirstWeekday

// Which day is day-month-year ?
private  int weekDay(int day, int month, int year) {
  return (FirstWeekday(year) + day - 1 +
     MONTH_COEFF[leapYear(year)][month]) % 7;
} // weekDay

// Number of Sundays fell on the first of the month
// during XX Century (1 Jan 1901 to 31 Dec 2000).
private void e19A() {
  int count = 0;
  for (int year = 1901; year <= 2000; ++year) {
    for (int month = 1; month <= 12; ++month) {
      if (weekDay(1,month,year) == SUNDAY) ++count;
    } // for month
  } // for year
  System.out.println( "\n Result e19A:  " + count);
} // e19A

// Number of Sundays fell on the first of the month
// during XX Century (1 Jan 1901 to 31 Dec 2000).
private void e19B() {
  int count = 0;
```

```
  for (int year = 1901; year <= 2000; ++year)
    count += numOfSun(year);
  System.out.println( "\n Result e19B:   " + count);
} // e19B

// Number of Sundays fell on the first of the month
// of the year
  private int numOfSun(int year) {
    int weekday = FirstWeekday(year), d = 0;
    int count = 0, v = 0;
    int leap = leapYear(year);
    for (int month = 1; month <= 12; ++month) {
      v = weekday + MONTH_COEFF[leap][month];
      if ((v == 0) || (v == 7)) ++count;
    } // for
    return count;
  } // numOfSun
} // class E19
```

The Month Coefficients

The *coefficient* of month m, $C(m)$, $1 \le m \le 12$ is the sum of all days before month m by modulo 7. If $N(i)$ is the number of days of month i then

$$C(m) = (N(1) + \ldots + N(m-1)) \bmod 7 \qquad (19.4)$$

$$1 \le m \le 12, \ N(0) = 0.$$

Denoted by $S(m)$ the sum of all days before month m, we have

$$S(m) = N(1) + \ldots + N(m-1)$$

So,

$$C(m) = S(m) \bmod 7$$

or

$$C(m) = (C(m-1) + N(m-1)) \bmod 7$$

$$C(0) = 0$$

The values of $C(m)$ depend only on the type of the year (common or leap). We temporarily use the notation $C_C(m)$ for the month coefficient of the common year and $C_L(m)$ for the month coefficient of the leap year.

If the given year is a common year, then $N(2) = 28$, and we have

$C_C(1) = N(0) \bmod 7 = 0$.

$C_C(2) = N(1) \bmod 7 = 31 \bmod 7 = 3$.

$C_C(3) = (C_C(2) + N(2)) \bmod 7 = (3 + 28) \bmod 7 = 3$.

$C_C(4) = (C_C(3) + N(3)) \bmod 7 = (3 + 31) \bmod 7 = 6$.

$C_C(5) = (C_C(4) + N(4)) \bmod 7 = (6 + 30) \bmod 7 = 1$.

$C_C(6) = (C_C(5) + N(5)) \bmod 7 = (1 + 31) \bmod 7 = 4$.

$C_C(7) = (C_C(6) + N(6)) \bmod 7 = (4 + 30) \bmod 7 = 6$.

$C_C(8) = (C_C(7) + N(7)) \bmod 7 = (6 + 31) \bmod 7 = 2$.

$C_C(9) = (C_C(8) + N(8)) \bmod 7 = (2 + 31) \bmod 7 = 5$.

$C(10) = (C_C(9) + N(9)) \bmod 7 = (5 + 30) \bmod 7 = 0$.

$C_C(11) = (C_C(10) + N(10)) \bmod 7 = (0 + 31) \bmod 7 = 3$.

$C_C(12) = (C_C(11) + N(11)) \bmod 7 = (3 + 30) \bmod 7 = 5$.

If the given year is a leap year, then $N(2) = 29$, and we have

$C_L(1) = N(0) \bmod 7 = 0$.

$C_L(2) = N(1) \bmod 7 = 31 \bmod 7 = 3$.

$C_L(3) = (C_L(2) + N(2)) \bmod 7 = (3 + 29) \bmod 7 = 4$.

$C_L(4) = (C_L(3) + N(3)) \bmod 7 = (4 + 31) \bmod 7 = 0$.

$C_L(5) = (C_L(4) + N(4)) \bmod 7 = (0 + 30) \bmod 7 = 2$.

$C_L(6) = (C_L(5) + N(5)) \bmod 7 = (2 + 31) \bmod 7 = 5$.

$C_L(7) = (C_L(6) + N(6)) \bmod 7 = (5 + 30) \bmod 7 = 0$.

$C_L(8) = (C_L(7) + N(7)) \bmod 7 = (0 + 31) \bmod 7 = 3$.

$C_L(9) = (C_L(8) + N(8)) \bmod 7 = (3 + 31) \bmod 7 = 6$.

$C_L(10) = (C_L(9) + N(9)) \bmod 7 = (6 + 30) \bmod 7 = 1$.

$C_L(11) = (C_L(10) + N(10)) \bmod 7 = (1 + 31) \bmod 7 = 4$.

$C_L(12) = (C_L(11) + N(11)) \bmod 7 = (4 + 30) \bmod 7 = 6$.

Since February of the leap year (29 days) is longer than February of the common year (28 days) one day, we get the following relation between coefficients of a month m of the leap year $C_L(m)$ and of the common year $C_C(m)$.

$$C_L(m) = C_C(m), \ 1 \leq m \leq 2$$
$$C_L(m) = (C_C(m) + 1) \bmod 7, \ 3 \leq m \leq 12.$$

Note

I believe that the readers can remember by heart all month coefficients of the common year. Because I am Vietnamese, my English is not enough to find an interesting clause for this. Here I try to give the following naïve clause

Oh(0) *tic*(3)-*tac*(3) *shift*(6) *one*(1) *for*(4) *showing*(6) *two*(2) *faces*(5) *or*(0) *three*(3) *faces*(5).

The next algorithm sets month coefficients to two-dimensional array C[][], where C[0][m] is coefficient of month m of a common year, and C[1][m] is coefficient of month m of a leap year.

```
Algorithm Month Coefficients
Input: t: 0...1; m: 1...12
Output: Month coefficient, C[t][m],
            t = 0 for common year,
            t = 1 for leap year,
            1 ≤ m ≤ 12.
begin
    C[0][1] ← C[1][1] ← 0;
    C[0](2) ← C[1][2] ← 3;
    for m ← 3 to 12 do
        C[0][m] ← (C[0][m-1] + N(m-1)) mod 7;
        // N(m) is the number of days of the month m
        // for common year
        C[1][m] ← (C[0][m]+1) mod 7;
    endfor m
    return  C[][]
endMonth Coefficiients
```

Example

We know that year 2018 has the first weekday w' = 1 (Monday), now we use the formula

$$\text{Weekday}(m) = (w' + C(m)) \bmod 7$$

to get the first weekday of all the rest months in year 2018 as follows.

Month	Jan	Feb	Mar	Apr	May	Jun	Jul	Aug	Sep	Oct	Nov	Dec
Code	1	2	3	4	5	6	7	8	10	10	11	12
Coeff	0	3	3	6	1	4	6	2	5	0	3	5
1st Wd	1	4	4	0	2	5	0	3	6	1	4	6
	Mon	Thu	Thu	Sun	Tue	Fri	Sun	Wed	Sat	Mon	Thu	Sat

The number of weekdays in a year

To improve the efficiency, we can initialize some values frequency using in the computation, for example, the number of weekdays in the year. Namely, we will set values to table ww[][][], where ww[0][w1][w] is the number of months in the year satisfying the conditions:

Common year (0)

The weekday of 1st Jan is w1

The weekday of 1st of the month is w

and ww[1][w1][w] is the number of months satisfying the conditions:

Leap year (1)

The weekday 1st Jan is w1

The weekday of 1st of the month is w

We know that the weekday of the first day of month m is $(w1 + C(m))$ mod 7. Using equation (19.3) with the right-side value w, we get a condition for finding the weekday w of the 1st - m.

$$(w1 + C(m)) \bmod 7 = w$$

```
Algorithm AllWeekdays
Input: non
Output: ww
begin
    Set ww ← all 0;
    for w1 ← 0 to 6 do
        // w1 is the first weekday of year
        // 0: Sun, 1: Mon, ..., 6: Sat
        for m ← 1 to 12 do
            // scan month 1...12
            add 1 to ww[0][w1][(w1 + C[0][m]) mod 7]; // for common year
            add 1 to ww[1][w1][(w1 + C[1][m]) mod 7]; // for leap yer
        end for m
    end for w1
    return ww
endAllWeekdays
```

Tab. 19.2 is a part of ww, ww[t][w1][w] and for all w1 = 0 (Sunday) to 6 (Saturday), w = 0 (Sunday), t = 0 (common year) and t = 1 (leap year).

Tab. **19.2** *The number of months having the 1st = Sunday*

	first weekday of the year (w')	0 Sun	1 Mon	2 Tue	3 Wed	4 Thu	5 Fri	6 Sat
Number of Sundays	Comm. year	2	2	2	1	3	1	1
	Leap year	3	2	1	2	2	1	1

Following to data in Tab. 19.2, we know that if the first weekday of a common year is Tuesday, then this year has 2 months having the 1st day = Sunday (1st-m = Sunday (0)), and if the first weekday of a leap year is Tuesday, then this year has 1 month having the 1st day = Sunday (1st-m = Sunday (0)).

Following the formula of the first weekday of the year we see that if the first weekday of year y is w then the first weekday of the next year y+1 will be (w+1) mod 7 if y is a common year, and (w+2) mod 7 if y is a leap year. After calling algorithms Month Coefficients and

AllWeekdays, we can construct a new version E19C for the Problem as follows.

```
Algorithm E19C
Input: Years 1901 – 2000
Output: Number of Sundays of 1-m, 1 ≤ m ≤ 12.
begin
    count ← 0;  Sunday ← 0;
    w1 ← FirstWeekDay(1901);
    for year ← 1901 to 2000 do
        if (LeapYear(year)) then
            add ly[w1][Sunday] to count; // ly: for leap year
            w1 ← (w1+2) mod 7;
        else
            add cy[w1][Sunday] to count; // cy: for common year
            w1 ← (w1+1) mod 7;
        endif
    endfor
    return count;
endE19C
```

The following programs include the features:

F1. Calculating the month coefficients, $C(m)$, 1 (January) $\leq m \leq 12$ (December), for common year and leap year.

F2. Calculating the numbers of weekdays for each given first weekday w1 of the year, 0 (Sunday) $\leq$ w, w1 ≤ 6 (Saturday).

F3. Giving a new version E19C for the Problem.

F4. Giving the month calendar for given month and year.

F5. Giving the year calendar for a given year.

F6. Giving the name of weekday of the given number day-month-year.

We will give a version E19C(year_start, year_end, wd) returning the number of weekdays wd on the first day of the month for the period from year_start to the year_end. That the answer of the Problem will be done after calling E19C(1901, 2000, 0);

C++ Program

```
/ * * * * * * * * * * * * * * * * * * * * * * * * * * * * * * * * * * * * * * * * * * * * * * * * * *
    Problem 19.
    F1. Calculating the month coefficients, C(m),
    1(January) ≤ m ≤ 12(December),
    for common year and leap year.
    F2. Calculating the numbers of weekday w
    for each given first weekday w1 of the year,
    0(Sunday) ≤ w, w1 ≤ 6 (Saturday).
    F3. Giving a new version E19C for the Problem,
    Answer = 171, Time = 0.09 sec.
    F4. Giving the month calendar for given month and
    year.
    F5. Giving the year calendar for a given year.
    F6. Giving the name of weekday of the given number
    day-month-year.
* * * * * * * * * * * * * * * * * * * * * * * * * * * * * * * * * * * * * * * * * * * * * * * * * * * /
#include <iostream>
#include <windows.h>
#include <math.h>

using namespace std;

/*-------------------------------------------------
    Some leap years (February has 29 days)
    1904, 1908, 1912, 1916, 1920, 1924, 1928, 1932,
    1936, 1940,1944, 1948, 1952, 1956, 1960, 1964,
    1968, 1972, 1976, 1980,1984, 1988, 1992, 1996,
    2000, 2004, 2008, 2012, 2016, 2020.
-------------------------------------------------*/

const int COMM = 0; // for commont year
const int LEAP = 1; // for leap year
const int SUN = 0; // Sunday
const int SAT = 6; // Saturday
const int JAN = 1;
const int FEB = 2;
const int DEC = 12;
```

```cpp
int NUM_DAY_OF_MONTH[2][13]=
{{0,31,28,31,30,31,30,31,31,30,31,30,31},//common year
{0,31,29,31,30,31,30,31,31,30,31,30,31}};//leap year

int MONTH_COEFF[2][13];
// values will be
// {{0,0,3,3,6,1,4,6,2,5,0,3,5},  //common year
// {0,0,3,4,0,2,5,0,3,6,1,4,6}};  //leap year

string MONTH_NAME[13] =
   {"","January","February","March","April",
   "May","June","July","August","September",
   "October","November", "December"};

string DAY_NAME[7] =
   {"Sunday","Monday","Tuesday","Wednesday",
   "Thursday","Friday","Saturday"};

char *STOP = "\n Press dot key (.) to stop: ";

int ww[2][7][7];
/*------------------------------------
   ww[0][w1][w]: number of weekdays
   w = 1-m if 1-Jan = w1 (common year)
   ww[1][w1][w]: number of weekdays
   w = 1-m if 1-Fan = w1(leap year)
-------------------------------------*/

void Go(const char * msg = STOP) {
   fflush(stdin);
   cout << msg;
   if (cin.get() =='.') exit(0);
} // Go

void MonthCoefficients() {
   MONTH_COEFF[COMM][JAN]=MONTH_COEFF[LEAP][JAN]=0;
   MONTH_COEFF[COMM][FEB]=MONTH_COEFF[LEAP][FEB]=31%7;
   for (int m = FEB+1; m <= DEC; ++m) {
      MONTH_COEFF[COMM][m]=(MONTH_COEFF[COMM][m-1]+
      NUM_DAY_OF_MONTH[COMM][m-1])%7;
      MONTH_COEFF[LEAP][m]=(MONTH_COEFF[COMM][m]+1)%7;
   } // for
} // MonthCoefficients
```

```
void AllWeekdays() {
  int w1, m;
  memset(ww, 0, sizeof(ww));
  for (w1 = SUN; w1 <= SAT; ++w1) {
    // w1 is the first weekday of year
  for (m = JAN; m <= DEC; ++m) {
    // scan month
    ++ww[COMM][w1][(w1+MONTH_COEFF[COMM][m])%7];
    ++ww[LEAP][w1][(w1+MONTH_COEFF[LEAP][m])%7];
  } // for m
} // for w1
} // AllWeekdays

bool LeapYear(int year) {
  // year = abcd
  int ab = year / 100;
  int cd = year - 100*ab;
  return (cd==0) ? ((ab%4)==0) : ((cd%4)==0);
} // LeapYear

// The first weekday of the year (Gauss)
// Sunday = 0, ..., Saturday = 6
int FirstWeekday(int year) {
  --year;
  return(1+5*(year%4)+4*(year%100)+6*(year%400))%7;
} // FirstWeekday

// Week day
int Weekday(int day, int month, int year) {
  return (FirstWeekday(year)
  +MONTH_COEFF[LeapYear(year)][month]+day-1)%7;
} // Weekday

// return the first day of month
// that is Sunday
int FindSunday(int month, int year) {
  return (1+(7-Weekday(1,month,year))%7);
} // FindSunday

string SayFirstWeekday(int year) {
  return DAY_NAME[FirstWeekday(year)];
} // SayFirstWeekday

string SayWeekday(int day, int month, int year) {
```

```
   return DAY_NAME[Weekday(day, month, year)];
} // SayWeekday

// Month Calendar
void MonthCalendar(int month, int year) {
   cout << "\n " << MONTH_NAME[month] << " " << year;
   cout << "    SUNDAY*" << endl;
   int t_year = LeapYear(year);
   int sd = FindSunday(month, year);
   int numDay = NUM_DAY_OF_MONTH[t_year][month];
   for (int day = 1; day <= numDay; ++day) {
     cout << " " << day;
     if (day == sd) { cout << "*"; sd += 7; }
   } // for
} // MonthCalendar

// Year Calendar
void YearCalendar(int year) {
   cout << "\n Calendar of " << year;
   for (int month = JAN; month <= DEC; ++month) {
     MonthCalendar(month, year); Go();
   } // for
} // YearCalendar

void E19C(int year_start, int year_end, int weekday) {
   int count = 0;
   int w1 =  FirstWeekday(year_start);
   for(int year=year_start;year<=year_end;++year) {
     if (LeapYear(year)) {
      count += ww[LEAP][w1][weekday];
      w1 = (w1+2) % 7;
     }
     else {
      count += ww[COMM][w1][weekday];
       w1 = (w1+1) % 7;
      }
     } // if
     cout << "\n E19C answer = " << count;
   } // E19C

// Shows the first weekdays of each year
// from 2010 to 2020
void Demo1() {
   for (int y = 2010; y <= 2020; ++y)
```

```cpp
    cout << "\n 1st Jan " << y << " is "
        << SayFirstWeekday(y);
} // Demo1

// Shows the weekdays of June 5th
// of each year from 2010 to 2020
void Demo2() {
  int d = 5, m = 6;
  for (int y = 2010; y <= 2020; ++y)
    cout << "\n " << d << " " << MONTH_NAME[m]
      << " " << y << " is " << SayWeekday(d,m,y);
} // Demo2

main() {
  // Init
  MonthCoefficients();
  AllWeekdays();
  E19C(1901, 2000, SUN); Go();
  Demo1(); Go();
  Demo2(); Go();
  MonthCalendar(5, 2018); Go();
  YearCalendar(2019);
  //-----------------------------
  cout << "\n  T H E    E N D .";
  return 0;
}
```

Free Pascal Program

```
(* * * * * * * * * * * * * * * * * * * * * * * * * * * * * * * * * * * * * * * * * * * * * * * * * * *
   Problem 19.
   F1. Calculating the month coefficients, C(m),
   1(January) ≤ m ≤ 12(December),
   for common year and leap year.
   F2. Calculating the numbers of weekday w
   for each given first weekday w1 of the year,
   0(Sunday) ≤ w, w1 ≤ 6 (Saturday).
   F3. Giving a new version E19C for the Problem,
   Answer = 171, , Time = 0.09 sec.
   F4. Giving the month calendar for given month and
   year.
   F5. Giving the year calendar for a given year.
   F6. Giving the name of weekday of the given number
   day-month-year.
```

```
*******************************************************)
uses crt; // for using readKey
(*-------------------------------------------------
   Some leap years (February has 29 days)
   1904, 1908, 1912, 1916, 1920, 1924, 1928, 1932,
   1936, 1940,1944, 1948, 1952, 1956, 1960, 1964,
   1968, 1972, 1976, 1980,1984, 1988, 1992, 1996,
  2000, 2004, 2008, 2012, 2016, 2020.
-------------------------------------------------*)

const NL = #13#10; BL = #32;
COMM = false; LEAP = true;
STOP = NL + ' Press dot key (.) to stop: ';
SUN = 0; SAT = 6;
JAN = 1; FEB = 2; DEC = 12;

type int = integer;
MFORM = array[COMM..LEAP,JAN..DEC] of int;
STR = string[20];

const

NUM_DAY_OF_MONTH: MFORM =
((31,28,31,30,31,30,31,31,30,31,30,31),//common year
(31,29,31,30,31,30,31,31,30,31,30,31));//leap year

MONTH_NAME: array[JAN..DEC] of STR =
('January','February','March','April',
'May','June','July','August','September',
'October','November', 'December' );

DAY_NAME: array[SUN..SAT] of STR =
('Sunday','Monday','Tuesday','Wednesday',
'Thursday','Friday','Saturday');

var

  MONTH_COEFF: MFORM;
  (* values will be
    ((0,3,3,6,1,4,6,2,5,0,3,5), // common year
    (0,3,4,0,2,5,0,3,6,1,4,6)); // leap year
  *)

  ww: array[COMM..LEAP,SUN..SAT,SUN..SAT] of int;
```

```
(*-------------------------------------
   ww[0][w1][w]: number of weekdays
   w = 1-m if 1-Jan = w1 (common year)
   ww[1][w1][w]: number of weekdays
   w = 1-m if 1-Fan = w1(leap year)
-------------------------------------*)

procedure Go(msg: string);
   var ch: char;
begin
   write(msg); ch := readKey;
   if ch = '.' then
   begin
     writeln(NL, 'Bye !');
     readln;
     halt;
   end;
end; // Go

procedure MonthCoefficients;
   var m: int;
begin
   MONTH_COEFF[COMM,JAN] := 0;
   MONTH_COEFF[LEAP,JAN] := 0;
   MONTH_COEFF[COMM,FEB] := 31 mod 7;
   MONTH_COEFF[LEAP,FEB] := 31 mod 7;
   for m := succ(FEB) to DEC do
   begin
     MONTH_COEFF[COMM,m] := (MONTH_COEFF[COMM,m-1]+
     NUM_DAY_OF_MONTH[COMM,m-1]) mod 7;
     MONTH_COEFF[LEAP,m]:=(MONTH_COEFF[COMM,m]+1)mod 7;
   end; // for
end; // MonthCoefficients

procedure AllWeekdays;
   var w1, m: int;
begin
   fillchar(ww, sizeof(ww), 0);
   for w1 := SUN to SAT do
   begin
     // w1 is the first weekday of year
     for m := JAN to DEC do
     begin // scan month
       inc(ww[COMM,w1, (w1+MONTH_COEFF[COMM,m])mod 7]);
```

```
      inc(ww[LEAP,w1,(w1+MONTH_COEFF[LEAP,m])mod 7]);
    end; // for m
  end; // for w1
end; // AllWeekdays

function LeapYear(year: int): Boolean;
  var ab, cd: int;
begin
  // year = ab|cd
    ab := year div  100; // 2 chu so dau
    cd := year mod 100; // 2 chu so cuoi
    if cd = 0 then exit(ab mod 4 = 0);
    exit(cd mod 4 = 0);
end; // LeapYear

function FirstWeekday(year: int): int; // Gauss
begin
  year := year - 1;
  exit((1+5*(year mod 4)+4*(year mod 100)
      + 6*(year mod 400)) mod 7);
end; // FirstWeekday

function WeekDay(day, month, year: int): int;
begin
  exit((FirstWeekday(year)
  + MONTH_COEFF[LeapYear(year),month]+day-1)mod 7);
end; // WeekDay

function SayFirstWeekday(year: int): string;
begin
  exit(DAY_NAME[FirstWeekday(year)]);
end; // SayFirstWeekday

function SayWeekday(day, mont, year: int): string;
begin
  exit(DAY_NAME[Weekday(day, mont, year)]);
end; // SayWeekday

// Find the first day in month
// that is Sunday
function FindSunday(month, year: int) : int;
begin
  FindSunday:=((7-Weekday(1,month,year)) mod 7)+1;
end; // FindSunday
```

```
procedure MonthCalendar(month, year: int);
   var day, sd: int;
begin
   write(NL, ' ', MONTH_NAME[month],' ', year);
   writeln('   SUNDAY*');
   sd := FindSunday(month, year);
   for day := 1 to
     NUM_DAY_OF_MONTH[LeapYear(year),month] do
     begin
       write(BL, day);
       if day = sd then
       begin write('*'); inc(sd, 7); end;
     end;
   end; // MonthCalendar

procedure YearCalendar(y: int);
   var m: int;
begin
   writeln(NL,'  Calendar of ', y);
   for m := JAN to DEC do
   begin
     MonthCalendar(m, y); Go(STOP);
   end;
end; // YearCalendar

procedure E19C(year_start, year_end, weekday: int);
   var count, w1, year: int;
begin
   count := 0;
   w1 :=  FirstWeekday(year_start);
   for year := year_start to year_end do
     if LeapYear(year) then
     begin
       inc(count, ww[LEAP,w1,weekday]);
       w1 := (w1+2) mod 7;
     end else
     begin
       inc(count, ww[COMM,w1,weekday]);
       w1 := (w1+1) mod 7;
     end;
   writeln(NL , ' E19C answer = ', count);
end; // E19C
```

```
// Shows the first weekdays of each year
// from 2010 to 2020
procedure Demo1;
   var y: int;
begin
   for y := 2010 to 2020 do
      writeln(NL,'  1st Jan ',y,' is ',
            SayFirstWeekday(y));
end; // Demo1

// Shows the weekdays of June 5th
// of each year from 2010 to 2020
procedure Demo2;
   var d, m, y: int;
begin
   d := 5; m := 6;
   for y := 2010 to 2020 do
      writeln(NL,BL,d,BL,MONTH_NAME[m], BL, y,' is ',
            SayWeekday(d, m, y));
end;

BEGIN
   MonthCoefficients;
   AllWeekdays;
   E19C(1901, 2000, SUN); Go(STOP);
   Demo1; Go(STOP);
   Demo2;  Go(STOP);
   MonthCalendar(5, 2018); Go(STOP);
   YearCalendar(2019);
   writeln(NL, '  T H E    E N D .');
   readln;
END.
```

Java Program

```
/************************************************
   Problem 19.
   F1. Calculating the month coefficients, C(m),
   1 (January) <= m <= 12 (December),
   for common year and leap year.
   F2. Calculating the numbers of weekday w
   for each given first weekday w1 of the year,
   0 (Sunday) <= w, w1 <= 6 (Saturday).
   F3. Giving a new version E19C for the Problem,
```

Answer = 171, Time = 0.09 sec.
F4. Giving the month calendar for given month and
year.
F5. Giving the year calendar for a given year.
F6. Giving the name of weekday of the given number
day-month-year.
Some leap years (February has 29 days)
1904, 1908, 1912, 1916, 1920, 1924, 1928, 1932,
1936, 1940,1944, 1948, 1952, 1956, 1960, 1964,
1968, 1972, 1976, 1980,1984, 1988, 1992, 1996,
2000, 2004, 2008, 2012, 2016, 2020.
**/

```java
import java.io.*;
import java.util.*;
public class E19 {
private int COMM = 0; // for common year
private int LEAP = 1; // for leap year
private int SUN = 0;
private int SAT = 6;
private int JAN = 1;
private int FEB = 2;
private int DEC = 12;

private int[][] NUM_DAY_OF_MONTH =
{{0,31,28,31,30,31,30,31,31,30,31,30,31},//common year
{0,31,29,31,30,31,30,31,31,30,31,30,31}};//leap year

private int[][] MONTH_COEFF = new int[2][13];
// values will be
// {{0,0,3,3,6,1,4,6,2,5,0,3,5}, // common year
// {0,0,3,4,0,2,5,0,3,6,1,4,6}}; // leap year

private int[][][] ww = new int [2][7][7];

private String[] MONTH_NAME =
{"","January","February","March","April",
"May","June","July","August","September",
"October","November", "December"};

private String[] DAY_NAME =
{"Sunday","Monday","Tuesday","Wednesday",
"Thursday","Friday","Saturday"};

E19() {
```

```java
      // Init
      monthCoefficients();
      allWeekdays();
      e19C(1901, 2000, SUN);       go();
      demo1(); go();
      demo2(); go();
      monthCalendar(5, 2018); go();
      yearCalendar(2019);
      System.out.println("\n  T H E    E N D .");
   }

private void go() {
   int c = 0;

   System.out.print("\n Press dot key [.] to stop\n"+
            " or other key to continue: ");
   try {
      c = System.in.read();
   }
   catch (IOException e){
      System.out.println();
   }
   if (c == '.') {
      System.out.println("\n Bye !");
      System.exit(0);
   }
} // Go

private void e19C(int year_start, int year_end,
            int weekday) {
   int count = 0;
   int w1 =  firstWeekday(year_start);
   for(int year=year_start;year<=year_end;++year) {
     if (leapYear(year) == LEAP) {
      count += ww[LEAP][w1][weekday];
      w1 = (w1+2) % 7;
      }
      else { count += ww[COMM][w1][weekday];
       w1 = (w1+1) % 7;
      } // if
   } // for
   System.out.println("\n E19C answer = "+count);
} // e19C
```

```
private String sayFirstWeekday(int year) {
   return DAY_NAME[firstWeekday(year)];
} // sayFirstWeekday

private String sayWeekday(int day,int month,int year){
   return DAY_NAME[weekday(day, month, year)];
} // sayWeekday

// Shows the first weekdays of each year
// from 2010 to 2020
private void demo1() {
   for (int y = 2010; y <= 2020; ++y)
   System.out.println("\n 1st Jan "+y+" is "
                      +sayFirstWeekday(y));
} // demo1

// Shows the weekdays of June 5th
// of each year from 2010 to 2020
private void demo2() {
   int d = 5, m = 6;
   for (int y = 2010; y <= 2020; ++y)
      System.out.println("\n "+d+" "+MONTH_NAME[m]
               +" "+y+" is "+sayWeekday(d, m, y));
} // demo2

private void monthCoefficients() {
   MONTH_COEFF[COMM][JAN]=MONTH_COEFF[LEAP][JAN]=0;
   MONTH_COEFF[COMM][FEB]=MONTH_COEFF[LEAP][FEB]=(31%7);
   for (int m = FEB+1; m <= DEC; ++m) {
      MONTH_COEFF[COMM][m] =
      (MONTH_COEFF[COMM][m-1]
      + NUM_DAY_OF_MONTH[COMM][m-1]) % 7;
      MONTH_COEFF[LEAP][m] = (MONTH_COEFF[COMM][m]
      + 1) % 7;
   } // for
} // monthCoefficients

private void allWeekdays() {
   int w1, m;
   for (int i = 0; i < 2; ++i)
      for (int j = 0; j < 7; ++j)
         for (int k = 0; k < 7; ++k)
            ww[i][j][k] = 0;
   for (w1 = SUN; w1 <= SAT; ++w1) {
```

```java
    // w1 is the first weekday of year
    for (m = JAN; m <= DEC; ++m) {
      // scan month
      ++ww[COMM][w1][(w1+MONTH_COEFF[COMM][m])%7];
      ++ww[LEAP][w1][(w1+MONTH_COEFF[LEAP][m])%7];
    } // for m
  } // for w1
} // allWeekday

private int leapYear(int year) {
  // year = abcd
  int ab = year / 100; // 2 first digits
  int cd = year - 100*ab; // 2 last digits
  if (cd == 0)
    return ((ab % 4) == 0) ? 1 : 0;
    // cd != 00
  return ((cd % 4) == 0) ? 1 : 0;
} // leapYear
private int firstWeekday(int year) {
  --year;
  return (1+5*(year%4)+4*(year%100)+6*(year%400))%7;
} // firstWeekday
private  int weekday(int day, int month, int year) {
  int d = firstWeekday(year) + day - 1;
  return (d+MONTH_COEFF[leapYear(year)][month])%7;
} // weekday

// return the first day of month
// that is Sunday
private int findSunday(int month, int year) {
  return (1 + (7-weekday(1, month, year)) % 7);
} // findSunday

// Month Calendar
private void monthCalendar(int month, int year) {
  System.out.println("\n "+MONTH_NAME[month]+" "+year);
  System.out.println("    SUNDAY* \n");
  int t_year = leapYear(year);
  int sd = findSunday(month, year);
  int numDays = NUM_DAY_OF_MONTH[t_year][month];
  for (int day = 1; day <= numDays; ++day){
    System.out.print(" " + day);
    if (day == sd) {
      System.out.print("*");
```

```
      sd += 7;
    }
  } // for
} // monthCalendar

private void yearCalendar(int y) {
  for (int month = JAN; month <= DEC; ++month) {
    monthCalendar(month, y);
    go();
  } // for
} // yearCalendar
} // class E19
```

Problem 20. Factorial digit sum

$n!$ means $n \times (n - 1) \times \ldots \times 3 \times 2 \times 1$. For example, $10! = 10 \times 9 \times \ldots \times 3 \times 2 \times 1 = 3628800$, and the sum of the digits in the number $10!$ is $3 + 6 + 2 + 8 + 8 + 0 + 0 = 27$.

Find the sum of the digits in the number $100!$

Algorithm

First, we need to organize an algorithm for calculating $n!$. This algorithm is similar to the algorithm 2^n in Problem 16. Let num[] be the array representing the big positive integer in the reversed form. Let Mult(c) be the function calculating num = num $\times$ c, where c is a 32 bits basic type integer. Let len be the number of digits of num. We multiply c by each digit of num as folows:

```
Algorithm Mult
Input: (num[], len).
integer c ≥ 0.
Output:  (num[], len), num = num × c
begin
    carry ← 0;
    for i ← 0 to len-1 do
        p ← c × num[i] + carry;
        carry ← p div 10;
        num[i] ← p – 10 × carry;
    endfor
    while (carry > 0) do
        p ← carry div 10;
        num[len] ← carry – 10 × p; // carry mod 10
        len ← len + 1;
        carry ← p;
    endwhile
    return (num[], len);
endMult
```

Then the factorial $n!$ is simple.

```
Algorithm Factorial
Input: integer n ≥ 0.
Output: num = n!.
begin
    set len ← 1
    set num[0] ← 1
    // 1! = 1, len(1!) = 1
    for c ← 2 to n do
        Mult(c);
    endfor
    return (num[], len);
endFactorial
```

Suppose we want to calculate num $= 11! = 10! \times 11$. After getting $10! = 3628800$, we need to do the last step 3628800×11 as follows.

position	0	1	2	3	4	5	6	7	
num[i]	0	0	8	8	2	6	3		10! = 3628800
p = 11×num[i]+carry	0	0	88	96	31	69	39		
new value of num[i]	0	0	8	6	1	9	9	3	
carry	0	0	8	9	3	6	3		

11! = 10! × 11 = 39916800.

Thus, $num[0...6] \times 11 = (0,0,8,8,2,6,3) \times 11 = (0,0,8,6,1,9,9,3) = num[0...7]$. The len is increased from 6 to 7.

To set the maximum size MN of the array num[] we need to evaluate the number of digits of 100!. We know that

$$n! = 1 \times 2 \times \dots \times n \leq n \times n \times \dots \times n = n^n$$

With $n = 100$ we get

$$\lg(100!) \leq \lg(100^{100}) = 100 \times \lg(10^2) = 200$$

where lg is $\log_{10}$

This boundary is too large. The running program found that MN = 158. After calculating 100! we take the sum of all the digits in num.

Algorithm E20
Input: integer n = 100
Output: sum of the digits in n!.
begin
Factorial(n); // num = n!
sum ← 0;
for each digit d in num do
sum ← sum + d;
endfor
return sum;
endE20

C++ Program

```
/************************************************
  Problem 20. Factorial digit sum
  Answer = 648, Time = 0.09 sec.
************************************************/
#include <iostream>

using namespace std;

const int MN = 160;

int num[MN];
int len; // number of digits

// num = c*num
void Mult(int c) {
  int carry = 0, i, p;
  for (i = 0; i < len; ++i) {
    p = c*num[i] + carry;
    carry = p / 10;
    num[i] = p - carry*10;
  } // for
  while (carry > 0) {
    p = carry / 10;
    num[len] = carry - p*10;
    ++len;
    carry = p;
  } // while
} // Mult
```

```cpp
void Factorial(int n) {
  len = 1; num[0] = 1;
  for (int i = 2; i <= n; ++i) Mult(i);
} // Factorial

void E20() {
  Factorial(100);
  int sum = 0;
  for (int i = 0; i < len; ++i)
    sum += num[i];
  cout << "\n Result: " << sum;
} // E20

main() {
  E20(); // 648
  cout << "\n  T H E    E N D .";
  return 0;
}
```

Free Pascal Program

```pascal
(* * * * * * * * * * * * * * * * * * * * * * * * * * * * * * * * * * * *
  Problem 20. Factorial digit sum
  Answer = 648, Time = 0.09 sec.
* * * * * * * * * * * * * * * * * * * * * * * * * * * * * * * * * * * * *)
const MN = 160; NL = #13#10; // new line

type int = integer;

var num: array[0..MN+1] of int;
len: int; // number of digits

// num = c*num
procedure Mult(c: int);
  var carry, p, i: int;
begin
  carry := 0;
  for i := 0 to len-1 do
  begin
   p := c*num[i] + carry;
   carry := p div 10;
   num[i] := p - 10*carry;
   end; // for
```

```
  while (carry > 0) do
  begin
   p := carry div 10;
   num[len] := carry - 10*p;
   inc(len);
   carry := p;
  end; // while
end; // Mult

procedure Factorial(n: int);
  var i: int;
begin
  len := 1; num[0] := 1; // 1! = 1, len(1!) = 1
  for  i := 2 to n do Mult(i);
end; // Factorial

procedure E20;
  var i, sum: int;
begin
  Factorial(100);
  sum := 0;
  for i := 0 to len-1 do
    sum := sum + num[i];
  writeln(NL, '  Result: ', sum);
end; // E20
BEGIN
  E20;  // 648
  writeln(NL, '  T H E    E N D .');
  readln;
END.
```

Java Program

The Java program below includes a variant using Java class BigInteger
(e20A).

```
/***********************************
  Problem 20. Factorial digit sum
  Answer = 648, Time = 0.09 sec.
*********************************/
import java.math.BigInteger;
import java.util.Arrays;
 public class E20 {
   static private int [] num = new int[200];
```

```
static private int len = 1;
E20() {
 e20A();
 e20B();
}

// Use BigInteger Class
private void e20A(){
 BigInteger f = BigInteger.valueOf(1);
 for (int i = 1; i <= 100; i++)
   f = f.multiply(BigInteger.valueOf(i));
 int sum = 0;
 String s = f.toString();
 for (int i = 0; i < s.length(); ++i) {
   sum += s.charAt(i)-'0';
 } // for
 System.out.println(sum);
} // e20A

// Make self
private void e20B(){
 len = 1; num[0] = 1; // 1! = 1, len(1!) = 1
 for (int c = 2; c <= 100; c++){
   Mult(c);
 } // for c
 int sum = 0;
 for (int i = 1; i < len; i++){
   sum += num[i];
 } // for i
 System.out.println(sum);
} // e20B

private void Mult(int c) {
 int carry = 0; // so nho carr
 int p = 0;
 for (int i = 0; i < len ; ++i) {
   p = c*num[i] + carry;
     carry = p / 10;
     num[i] = p - 10*carry;
   } // for i
   while (carry != 0) {
     p = carry / 10;
     num[len++] = carry - 10*p;
     carry = p;
```

```
      } // while
   } // e20B
} // E20
```

Comment

C1. Note that 10^{24} is a factor of 100!, so 100! is ended with 24 zero. Therefore, we can ignore computing multiplication by 10^{24}. To show $10^{24} \mid 100!$ we denote by Deg(p, n) the greatest integer k that $p^k \mid n!$, where p is a prime and n is a positive integer. For example, if $n = 10$ then we have

$$n! = 1 \times 2 \times 3 \times 4 \times 5 \times 6 \times 7 \times 8 \times 9 \times 10 = 2^8 \times 3^4 \times 5^2 \times 7$$

so Deg(2, 10) = 8, Deg(3, 10) = 4, Deg(5, 10) = 2, Deg(7, 10) = 1, and for any other prime p, we have Deg(p, n) = 0. Now, we can write $n!$ as

$$n! = a \times 2^6 \times (2 \times 5)^2 = a \times 2^6 \times 10^2$$

This decomposition of $n!$ shows that 10! is ended with two zero.

In any five consecutive positive integers, there are as least two even number and only one multiple of five. This implies Deg(5, n) < Deg(2, n). In the other hand, $2 \times 5 = 10$, therefore, for any positive number n, the number of the last zero of $n!$ is Deg(5, n).

For a given prime p and a positive integer n, if we write the product $n! = 1 \times 2 \times \ldots \times n$ in the lines with p numbers per line, then we get $k = n$ div p full lines. The last terms of these lines are $1 \times p$, $2 \times p$,..., $k \times p$, and their product is $k! \times p^k$. Now, in the product $k! = 1 \times 2 \times \ldots \times k$, we again find k div p terms of the form $i \times p$, $1 \leq i \leq k$ div p. Therefore, function Deg(p, n) can be defined recursively as follows:

Deg(p, 0) = 0.

Deg(p, n) = (n div p) + Deg(p, n div p), $n > 0$.

The next algorithm gives Deg(p, n) in a non-recursive form.

```
Algorithm Deg
Input: prime p, integer n.
Output: Greatest integer k: p^k | n!.
begin
    k ← 0
    while (n ≠ 0) do
        n ← n div p;
        k ← k + n;
    endwhile
    return k;
endDeg
```

The next examples demonstrate how to get Deg(2,100) and Deg(5,100).

100 div 2	=	50		100 div 5	=	20
50 div 2	=	25	Deg(2, 100) = 97,	20 div 5	=	4
25 div 2	=	12	Deg(5, 100) = 24.	4 div 5	=	0
12 div 2	=	6		Deg(5, 100)	=	24
6 div 2	=	3				
3 div 2	=	1				
1 div 2	=	0				
Deg(2, 100)	=	97				

C2. Let a and b be natural numbers below constant $M = 101$, and num be a big integer with the len digits. We temporally call $a \times b$ a *small multiplication* (abbreviated to SM) and num $\times a$ a *large multiplication* (abbreviated to LM). Then two next program segments A and B give the same value of num, but they are not equivalent by the computational times.

The segment A calculates (num $\times a$) $\times b$ with two LMs. The segment B calculates num $\times (a \times b)$ with one SM and one LM.

A	B
`num = num × a;` `num = num × b;`	`v = a × b` `num = num × v;`

Each operation num × x needs len SMs and len additions generated by carries. Therefore, the segment A needs 2×len SMs and 2×len additions. The segment B needs len+1 SMs and len additions. We say that the segment B executes faster than the segment A about 2 times.

Now we apply remarks C1 and C2 above to the computation of 100! = $1 \times 2 \times \ldots \times 100$ as follows. At each step, we take two numbers x and y from the left and the right sides of the sequence 1, 2, …, 99, 100. Let $x = u2^a5^b$ and $y = v2^c5^d$ where $a = \text{Deg}(2, x)$, $b = \text{Deg}(5, x)$, $c = \text{Deg}(2, y)$ and $d = \text{Deg}(5, y)$. Let $z = u \times v$. We calculate num = num × z and accumulate a, c to deg2 (a counting variable of Deg(2, 100)) and b, d to deg5 (a counting variable of Deg(5, 100)).

In general, for any positive integer n, $n!$ can be written as follows:

$$n! = 2^{deg2}5^{deg5}\prod_{i=1}^{n}d_i = 2^{deg2-deg5}10^{deg5}\prod_{i=1}^{n}d_i \qquad (20.1)$$

$$deg2 = \sum_{i=1}^{n}a, \qquad deg5 = \sum_{i=1}^{n}b,$$

$$i = d_i2^a5^b, a = Deg(2,i), b = Deg(5,i)$$

Thus, we can use formula (20.1) to organize an algorithm for computing $n!$ as follows.

$$n! = A \times B \times C \qquad (20.2)$$

$$A = \prod_{i=1}^{n}d_i$$

$$B = 2^{deg2-deg5} = ShiftLeft(1, deg2 - deg5)$$

$$C = 10^{deg5}$$

where algorithm ShiftLeft for computing num $\times 2^k$ is given in Problem 16.

Algorithm FactorialB

Input: positive integer n.
Output: n!
begin
    set len ← 1; set num[0] ← 1;
    // (num, len) = 1!
    deg2 ← 0; deg5 ← 0;
    i ← 1; j ← n;
    while (i < j) do
        x ← i; y ← j;
        factorize x = $u2^a5^b$;
        factorize y = $v2^c5^d$;
        Mult(u×v) // num = num × u × v
        deg2 ← deg2 + a + c;
        deg5 ← deg5 + b + d;
        i ← i + 1; j ← j − 1;
    endwhile
    // i = j
    Mult(i);
    diff ← deg2 - deg5;
    set k ← 25;
    while (diff > k) do
        ShiftLeft(k);
        diff ← diff − k;
    endwhile
    ShiftLeft(diff);
    return (num[], len);
endFactorialB

Since we need to get sum of digits of $n!$, we can ignore part C in (20.2). Now algorithm E20B can be represented as follows:

Algorithm E20B
Input: integer n = 100
Output: sum of the digits in n!.
begin
FactorialB(n); // num = n!
sum ← 0;
for each digit d in num do
sum ← sum + d;
endfor
return sum;
endE20B

C++ Program

```
/*************************************
  Problem 20. Factorial digit sum
  Version E20B
  Answer = 648, Time = 0.07 sec.
*************************************/
#include <iostream>
using namespace std;
const int MN = 160;
int num[MN];
int len; // number of digits

// num = c*num
void Mult(int c) {
  int carry = 0, i, p;
  for (i = 0; i < len; ++i) {
    p = c*num[i] + carry;
    carry = p / 10;
    num[i] = p - carry*10;
  } // for
  while (carry > 0) {
    p = carry / 10;
    num[len] = carry - p*10;
    ++len;
    carry = p;
  } // while
} // Mult

// num = num * (2^k)
void ShiftLeft(int k) {
```

```
  int c = 0, d;
  for (int i = 0; i < len; ++i) {
   num[i] = (num[i] << k) + c;
   //num[i] = num[i]*(2^k)+c
   c = num[i] / 10;
   num[i] -= c*10;
  } // for
  while (c > 0) {
   d = c / 10;
   num[len++] = c - d*10;
   c = d;
  } // while
} // ShiftLeft

  // n!/10^deg5
  void FactorialB(int n) {
   int deg = 0; // deg2 = 97 > deg5 = 24
     // deg = deg2 - deg5
   int i, j;
   len = 1; num[0] = 1;
   int k = 25;
   int x, y;
   // factorial
   for (i = 2, j = n; i < j; ++i, --j) {
     x = i; y = j;
     while (x % 2 == 0) { x /= 2; ++deg; }
     while (x % 5 == 0) { x /= 5; --deg; }
     while (y % 2 == 0) { y /= 2; ++deg; }
     while (y % 5 == 0) { y /= 5; --deg; }
     Mult(x*y);
   } // for i
   x = i; Mult(x);
   // num = num*(2^deg)
   while (deg >= k) {
     ShiftLeft(k); // num = num*(2^25)
     deg -= k;
   } // while deg
   ShiftLeft(deg);
  } // FactorialB

  void E20B() {
   FactorialB(100);
   int sum = 0;
   for (int i = 0; i < len; ++i)
```

```
   sum += num[i];
  cout << "\n Result: " << sum;
  } // E20B

  main() {
     E20B();
     cout << "\n  T H E    E N D .";
     return 0;
  }
```

Free Pascal Program

```
(*************************************
  Problem 20. Factorial digit sum
  Version E20B
  Answer = 648, Time = 0.07 sec.
*************************************)

const MN = 160; NL = #13#10;
type int = longint;
var
  num: array [1..MN] of int;
  len : int; // number of digits

// num := c*num
procedure Mult(c: int);
  var carry, i, p: int;
begin
  carry := 0;
  for i := 1 to len do
  begin
    p := c*num[i] + carry;
    carry := p div 10;
    num[i] := p - carry*10;
  end; // for
  while (carry > 0) do
  begin
    inc(len);
    p := carry div 10;
    num[len] := carry - p*10;
    carry := p;
  end; // while
end; // Mult
```

```
// num := num * (2^k)
procedure ShiftLeft(k: int);
 var c, d, i: int;
begin
 c := 0;
 for i := 1 to len do
 begin
  num[i] := (num[i] shl k) + c;
  //num[i] := num[i]*(2^k) + c
  c := num[i] div 10;
   dec(num[i], c*10);
  end; // for
  while (c > 0) do
  begin
   d := c div 10;
   inc(len);
   num[len] := c - d*10;
   c := d;
  end; // while
 end; // ShiftLeft

 // n! div 10^deg5
 procedure FactorialB(n: int);
 var deg: int; // deg2 := 97 > deg5 := 24
                // deg = deg2 - deg5
   i, j, k: int;
   x, y: int;
 begin
   deg := 0;
   len := 1; num[1] := 1;
   k := 25;
   i := 2; j := n;
   while (i < j) do
   begin
    x := i; y := j;
    while (x mod 2 = 0) do
    begin
     x := x div 2;
     inc(deg)
    end; // while x mod 2
    while (x mod 5 = 0) do
    begin
     x := x div 5;
     dec(deg)
```

```
      end; // while x mod 5
      while (y mod 2 = 0) do
      begin
        y := y div 2;
        inc(deg)
      end; // while y mod 2
      while (y mod 5 = 0) do
      begin
        y := y div 5;
        dec(deg)
      end; // while y mod 5
        Mult(x*y);
        inc(i); dec(j);
    end; //while i < j
 x := i; Mult(x);
 // num := num*(2^deg)
 while (deg >= k) do
 begin
   ShiftLeft(k); // num := num*(2^25)
   deg := deg - k;
 end; // while x
 ShiftLeft(deg);
end; // FactorialB

procedure E20B;
 var sum, i : int;
begin
 FactorialB(100);
 sum := 0;
 for i := 1 to len do
   inc(sum, num[i]);
 writeln(NL, sum);
end; // E20B

BEGIN
   E20B;
   writeln(NL, '  T H E   E N D .');
   readln;
END.
```

Java Program

```
/**********************************
   Problem 20. Factorial digit sum
```

```
   Version E20B
   Answer = 648, Time = 0.07 sec.
   ********************************* /
import java.math.BigInteger;
import java.util.Arrays;

public class E20 {
  static private int [] num = new int[160];
  static private int len = 1;

    E20() {
      E20B();
    }

  // num = c*num
  private void Mult(int c) {
   int carry = 0, i, p;
   for (i = 0; i < len; ++i) {
     p = c*num[i] + carry;
     carry = p / 10;
     num[i] = p - carry*10;
   } // for i
   while (carry > 0) {
     p = carry / 10;
     num[len] = carry - p*10;
     ++len;
     carry = p;
   } // while carry
  } // Mult

  // n! / 10^deg5
  private void FactorialB(int n) {
    int deg = 0; // deg2 = 97 > deg5 = 24
                 // deg = deg2-deg5
    int i, j;
    int k = 25;
    int x, y;
    len = 1; num[0] = 1;
    // factorial
    for (i = 2, j = n; i < j; ++i, --j) {
      x = i; y = j;
      while (x % 2 == 0) { x /= 2; ++deg; }
      while (x % 5 == 0) { x /= 5; --deg; }
      while (y % 2 == 0) { y /= 2; ++deg; }
```

```
      while (y % 5 == 0) { y /= 5; --deg; }
      Mult(x*y);
  } // for
  x = i; Mult(x);
  // num = num*(2^deg)
  while (deg >= k) {
    ShiftLeft(k); // num = num*(2^25)
    deg -= k;
  } // while deg >= k
  ShiftLeft(deg);
  }// FactorialB

  private void E20B() {
    int sum = 0;
    FactorialB(100);
    for (int i = 0; i < len; ++i)
      sum += num[i];
    System.out.println("\n Result: " + sum);
  }// E20B

  void ShiftLeft(int k) {
    int c = 0, d;
    for (int i = 0; i < len; ++i) {
      num[i] = (num[i] << k) + c;
      //num[i] = num[i]*(2^k) + c
      c = num[i] / 10;
      num[i] -= c*10;
    } // for
    while (c > 0) {
      d = c / 10;
      num[len++] = c - d*10;
      c = d;
    } // while c
  }  // ShiftLeft
} // E20
```

Problem 21. Amicable numbers

Let $d(n)$ be defined as the sum of proper divisors of n (numbers less than n which divide evenly into n). If $d(a) = b$ and $d(b) = a$, where $a \neq b$, then a and b are an *amicable pair* and each of a and b are called *amicable numbers*. For example, the proper divisors of 220 are 1, 2, 4, 5, 10, 11, 20, 22, 44, 55 and 110; therefore $d(220) = 284$. The proper divisors of 284 are 1, 2, 4, 71 and 142; so $d(284) = 220$.

Evaluate the sum of all the amicable numbers under 10000.

Algorithm

Step 1. Compute the sum of all proper divisors of i for all i, $d(i)$, $1 \leq i <$ MN = 10000. We construct a similar algorithm to Sieve of Eratosthenes (see Problem 7) as follows. For each natural number i from 2 to 9999 div 2, we consider i as a divisor of all numbers $k \times i$ between $2 \times i$ and 9999, so we add i to the $d[k \times i]$.

```
Algorithm Setd
Input: integer MN = 10000.
Output: d[1...MN−1].
        d[i] = sum {a | a < i, i = k×a, 1 ≤ i ≤ MN−1}
begin
   d[1] ← 0;
   set d[i] ← 1, 1 ≤ i < MN;
   // 1 is a proper divisor of all i > 1
   for i ← 2 to (MN−1) div 2 do
      for j ← (i + i) to MN−1 step i do
         d[j] ← d[j] + i;
      endfor j
   endfor i
   return d[];
endSetd
```

Note that if a is prime then $d(a) = 1$, so all primes are not amicable numbers.

Step 2. Let (a, b) be an amicable pair. Since $b \neq a$ we can suppose $a < b$. Therefore, to find (a, b), we scan each number a from 2 to MN−1 and verify the following conditions:

- $b = d[a]$
- $a < b < MN$
- $d[b] = a$

If all these conditions are satisfied, then (a, b) is an amicable pair, and a and b must be added to the final sum. To eliminate repeated numbers, we set a mark to this pair. Since $a < b$ we need to mark only b by setting $d[b] = 1$.

```
Algorithm E21
Input: integer MN = 10000.
Output: sum {a+b | 1 ≤ a < b < MN, d(a) = b, d(b) = a}
begin
    Setd;
    sum ← 0;
    for a ← 2 to MN-1 do
        b ← d[a];
        if (a < b and b < MN and d[b] = a) then
            add (a+b) to sum;
            d[b] ← 1; // mark b to be added
        endif
    endfor
    return sum;
endE21
```

C++ Program

```
/*******************************************************
    Problem 21. Amicable numbers
    sum{ (a+b)|a < b < 10000,d(a)=b,d(b)= a}
    Answer = 31626, Time = 0.12 sec.
*******************************************************/
#include <iostream>
#include <windows.h>
```

```
using namespace std;

  const int MN = 10000;
  int d[MN+1];

  // d[j] = sum {i| i < j, i divides j}
  // 1 <= j < 10000.
  void Setd() {
    int i, j, n2 = MN/2;
    d[0] = d[1] = 0;
    for(i = 2; i < MN; ++i) d[i] = 1; // Init all 1
    for(i = 2; i <= n2; ++i) {
     for (j = i+i; j <= MN; j += i) {
       // j = k*i -> i divides j
       d[j] += i;
         // d[j] = sum {i| i < j, i divides j}
      } // for j
    } // for i
    // max(d[i]) = 25320; imax = 9240
  } // Set d

  void E21() {
    int a, b, sum = 0;
    Setd();
    for (a = 2; a < MN; ++a) {
     if (d[a] > 1) {
       b = d[a];
       if (a < b && b < MN) {
         if (d[b] == a) {
          sum += (a + b);
          d[b] = 1; // Mark b to be used
         } // if d[b]
       } // if b
     } // if d[a]
    } // for a
   cout << "\n " << sum;
  } // E21

  main() {
    E21(); // 31626
    cout << "\n  T H E    E N D .";
    return 0;
  }
```

Free Pascal Program

```
(*****************************************************
   Problem 21. Amicable numbers
   sum{(a+b)|a < b < 10000,d(a)=b,d(b)= a}
  Answer = 31626, Time = 0.12 sec.
*****************************************************)
const MN = 10000; NL = #13#10;
type int = longint;
var
  d: array[1..MN] of int;

// d[j] = sum {i| i < j, i divides j}
// 1 <= j < 10000.
procedure Setd;
  var i, j, n2 : int;
begin
  d[1] := 0;
  n2 := MN div 2;
  for i := 2 to MN-1 do d[i] := 1; // Init all 1
  for i := 2 to n2 do
  begin
    j := i + i;
    while (j <= MN)do
    begin
     // j = k*i -> i divides j
     d[j] := d[j] + i;
     // d[j] = sum {i| i < j, i divides j}
     j := j + i;
    end; // whille
  end; // for i
  // max(d[i]) = 25320; imax = 9240
end; // Setd

procedure E21;
  var a, b, sum: int;
begin
  sum := 0;
  Setd;
  for a := 2 to MN-1 do
    if (d[a] > 1) then
    begin
```

```
      b := d[a];
      if (a < b) and (b < MN) then
      begin
        if (d[b] = a) then
        begin
          sum := sum + a + b;
          d[b] := 1; // mark b as used
        end; // if d
      end; // if a < b…
    end; // for a
    writeln(NL, sum);
  end; // E21

  BEGIN
    E21; // 31626
    writeln(NL, ' T H E    E N D .');
    readln;
  END.
```

Java Program

```
/************************************************
   Problem 21. Amicable numbers
   sum{ (a+b) |a < b < 10000, d(a)=b, d(b)= a}
   Answer = 31626, Time = 0.12 sec.
*************************************************/
import java.util.BitSet;
public class E21{
  private int MN = 10000;
  private int d[] = new int[MN+1];

  E21(){
   int a, b, sum = 0;
   Setd();
   for (a = 2; a < MN; ++a)
    if (d[a] > 1){
       b = d[a];
       if (b < MN){
         if (a < b){
          if (d[b] == a) {
           sum += (a + b);
           d[b] = 1; // mark b as used
          } // if d[b]
         } // if a < b
```

```
        } // if b < MN
      } // if d[a] > 1
   System.out.println("\n " + sum); // 31626
   } // E21

   // d[j] = sum {i| i < j, i divides j}
   // 1 <= j < 10000.
   void Setd() {
      int i = 0, j = 0;
      d[0] = d[1] = 0;
      int n2 = MN / 2;
      for (i = 2; i < MN; ++i) d[i] = 1;//set d all 1
      for (i = 2; i <= n2; ++i) {
        for (j = i + i; j < MN; j += i){
          // j = k*i -> i divides j
          d[j] += i;
            // d[j] = sum {i| i < j, i divides j}
        } // for j
      } // for i
   } // setd
} // class E21
```

Problem 22. Names scores

Using names.txt (right click and 'Save Link/Target As...'), a 46K text file containing over five-thousand first names, begin by sorting it into alphabetical order. Then working out the alphabetical value for each name, multiply this value by its alphabetical position in the list to obtain a name score.

For example, when the list is sorted into alphabetical order, COLIN, which is worth 3 + 15 + 12 + 9 + 14 = 53, is the 938th name in the list. So, COLIN would obtain a score of 938 × 53 = 49714.

What is the total of all the name scores in the file?

Algorithm

Step 1. Download file po22_names.txt.

Right click and 'Save Link/Target As...' you will get a file named "p022_names.txt" in your hard disk of your computer. This text file p022_names.txt contains over five-thousand first names. In your programming environment, you can read and observe the content of this file to understand its structure. Here is the first segment of the file:

```
"MARY","PATRICIA","LINDA","BARBARA","ELIZABETH","JENNIFER",
"MARIA","SUSAN","MARGARET","DOROTHY","LISA","NANCY","KAREN",
"BETTY","HELEN","SANDRA","DONNA","CAROL","RUTH","SHARON",
"MICHELLE","LAURA","SARAH","KIMBERLY","DEBORAH","JESSICA",
"SHIRLEY","CYNTHIA","ANGELA","MELISSA","BRENDA","AMY","ANNA",
"REBECCA","VIRGINIA","KATHLEEN","PAMELA","MARTHA","DEBRA",
"AMANDA","STEPHANIE","CAROLYN","CHRISTINE","MARIE","JANET",
"CATHERINE","FRANCES","ANN","JOYCE","DIANE","ALICE","JULIE",
"HEATHER","TERESA","DORIS","GLORIA","EVELYN","JEAN","CHERYL",
"MILDRED","KATHERINE","JOAN","ASHLEY","JUDITH","ROSE","JANICE",
"KELLY","NICOLE","JUDY","CHRISTINA","KATHY","THERESA","BEVERLY"
,"DENISE","TAMMY","IRENE","JANE","LORI","RACHEL","MARILYN",
"ANDREA","KATHRYN","LOUISE","SARA","ANNE","JACQUELINE","WANDA",
"BONNIE","JULIA","RUBY","LOIS","TINA","PHYLLIS","NORMA","PAULA"
,"DIANA","ANNIE","LILLIAN","EMILY","ROBIN","PEGGY","CRYSTAL",
"GLADYS","RITA","DAWN","CONNIE","FLORENCE","TRACY","EDNA",
"TIFFANY","CARMEN","ROSA","CINDY","GRACE","WENDY","VICTORIA",
"EDITH","KIM","SHERRY","SYLVIA","JOSEPHINE","THELMA","SHANNON",
"SHEILA"...
```

File formatting

The names are written in double quotes (") and separated by a comma (,).

Step 2. Names splitting. Open file po22_names.txt and read each name to the array names[] of string, and count the number of reading elements to the variable n.

For each character c read from file po22_names.txt, we distinguish three cases:

- c is in {'A', ..., 'Z'}: Append c to the current name.

- c is a double quote ("): Double quote is used in two cases:

- At the beginning of a new name, for example, "COLIN".

- At the end of the name, for example, "COLIN".

So we use a *state variable* to distinguish these cases. We set state = 1 if we meet 'A' to 'Z' and set state = 0 if c is outside of {'A', ..., 'Z'}

name	"	C	O	L	I	N	"	,
state	0	1	1	1	1	1	0	0

- c is a comma (,): Ignore.

Algorithm Read file
Input: file "po22_names.txt" (saved in disk)
Output: array names[1...n]

```
begin                                          * case state = 1:
    open file f with name "po22_names.txt" ;       if (c is in ALPHA) then
    n ← 0; // name counting                        // continue to get name
    ALPHA ← {'A', ..., 'Z'};                       append c to names[n];
    state ← 0; // outside of ALPHA                 else // outside of ALPHA
    while (not end of file f) do                   // end of names[n]:
        read the next character c from f ;         // close names[n]
        select one of the following cases:         state ← 0;
        * case state = 0 :                         // change state to 0
            if (c is in ALPHA) then                end if c
            // meet a new name                  end case state = 1
                n ← n + 1;                   end select
                append c to names[n];        end while
                state ← 1; // inside ALPHA   close f;
            endif c;                         end Read file.
        end case state = 0;
```

Step 3. Sort array names[] into alphabetical order.

We construct an algorithm for quick sorting the array names[] by indexes. The algorithm does not move the objects (names) in the array names[]. An array id[] is used to point to the positions of the objects in the array names[]. This approach ignores all the names copy operations in the given array.

	id			names []
1	4		1	MARY
2	5		2	PATRICIA
3	6		3	LINDA
4	3		4	BARBARA
5	1		5	ELIZABETH
6	2		6	JENNIFER

```
id[1] = 4; names[id[1]] = names[4] = "BARBARA".
id[2] = 5; names[id[2]] = names[5] = "ELIZABETH".
id[3] = 6; names[id[3]] = names[6] = "JENNIFER".
id[4] = 3; names[id[4]] = names[3] = "LINDA".
id[5] = 1; names[id[5]] = names[1] = "MARY".
id[6] = 2; names[id[6]] = names[2] = "PATRICIA".
```

```
Algorithm Sort
Input: names[1...n], id[1...n].
Output: ALPHA sorted names[1...n] by id
begin
    initialize id: id[i] ← i, 1 ≤ i ≤ n;
    IdQuickSort(1, n);
    return id;
end Sort.
```

```
Algorithm IdQuickSort(d, c)
Input: names[d...c], id[].
Output: ALPHA sorted names[d...c] by indexes id[d...c]
begin
    m ← id[(d+c) div 2];
    i ← d; j ← c;
    while (i ≤ j) do
        while (names[i] < names[m]) do i ← i + 1 endwhile;
        while (names[m] < names[j]) do j ← j - 1 endwhile;
        if (i ≤ j) then
            Swap(id[i], id[j]);
            i ← i + 1; j ← j - 1;
        endif
    endwhile
    if (d < j) then IdQuickSort(d, j) endif;
    if (i < c) then IdQuickSort(i, c) endif;
end IdQuickSort.
```

Step 4. For each name s = names[i] in the alphabetical sorted array names[] we calculate the score of s by the following formula:

$$Score(s) = i \times \sum_{j=1}^{\#s} Code(s_j)$$

where

i is the order of name s in the sorted array names[] beginning from 1.

$\#s$ is the number of characters in $s = s_1 \ldots s_\#$.

$Code('A') = 1$, $Code('B') = 2$, $\ldots$, $Code('Z') = 26$.

The final result of the Problem is sum{ $Score(s) \mid s \in$ names}

$$\sum_{i=1}^{n} Score(names[i])$$

C++ Program

```
/********************************************
    Problem 22. Names Scores
    Answer = 871198282, Time = 0.02 sec.
*********************************************/
#include <iostream>
#include <fstream>
#include <windows.h>

using namespace std;

typedef char str[12];

const int MN = 6000;
const char * FN = "p022_names.txt";

#define ALPHA(c) (c >= 'A' && c <= 'Z')

str names[MN];
int id[MN];
int n;

void ReadInput() {
    char c;
    int state;
    int i;
    ifstream f(FN);
    if (f.fail()) {
        cout << "\n Unable open input file " << FN;
        exit(1);
    } // if
    state = 0; // Outside of ALPHA
    n = 0; // index of names[]
    while (f >> c) { // read the next char c
        switch(state) {
            case 0: // Not ALPHA
                if (!ALPHA(c)) break;
                // meet a new name
                i = 0;
                names[++n][i++] = c;
                state = 1;
                break;
            case 1: // ALPHA
```

```
            if (ALPHA(c)) {
               names[n][i++] = c; break;
            }
            names[n][i] = '\0'; // close names[n]
            state = 0; // change state to 0
            break;
      } // switch
   } // while
   f.close();
} // ReadInput

void IdQuickSort(int d, int c) {
   int i = d, j = c, m = id[(d+c)/2], t;
   while (i <= j) {
      while (strcmp(names[id[i]], names[m]) < 0) ++i;
      while (strcmp(names[m], names[id[j]]) < 0) --j;
      if (i <= j) {
         t = id[i];
         id[i] = id[j];
         id[j] = t;
         ++i; --j;
      } // if
   } // while i <= j
   if (d < j) IdQuickSort(d,j);
   if (i < c) IdQuickSort(i,c);
} // IdQuickSort

int CodeSum(str s) {
   int sum = 0;
   for (int i = 0; s[i]; ++i)
    sum += s[i]-'A'+1;
   return sum;
} // CodeSum

void E22() {
   int i, score;
   ReadInput();
   for (i = 1; i <= n; ++i) id[i] = i;
   IdQuickSort(1,n);
   score = 0;
   for (i = 1; i <= n; ++i) {
    score += i*CodeSum(names[id[i]]);
   } // for
   cout << "\n Total Score: " << score;
```

```
} // E22

main() {
  E22(); // 871198282
  // ----------------------------
  cout << "\n  T H E    E N D .";
  return 0;
}
```

Free Pascal Program

```
(*********************************************
   Problem 22. Names Scores
   Answer = 871198282, Time = 0.02 sec.
*********************************************)
type str = string[12];
int = longint;
const  MN = 6000; NL = #13#10;
FN = 'p022_names.txt'; // file name
var
  names: array[0..MN] of str;
  id: array[0..MN] of int;
  n: int ; // index of names

// c is in {'A',...,'Z'}
function Alpha(c: char): boolean;
begin
  exit((c >= 'A') and (c <= 'Z'));
end; // Alpha

procedure ReadInput;
var
  c: char;
  state: int;
  i: int;
  f: text;
begin
  // Set all names empty
  for i := 1 to MN do names[i] := '';
  assign(f, FN); reset(f);
  state := 0; // Outside of ALPHA
  n := 0; // index of names
  while not eof(f) do
  begin
```

```
    read(f,c);
    case state of
      0: // Not ALPHA
        if ALPHA(c) then
        begin // meet a new name
          inc(n);
          names[n] := names[n] + c;
          state := 1; // Inside of ALPHA
        end;
       1: // ALPHA
         if (ALPHA(c)) then
           names[n] := names[n] + c
         else  state := 0;
    end; // case
  end; // while
  close(f);
end; // ReadInput

procedure IdQuickSort(d, c: int);
  var  i, j, m, t: int;
begin
  i := d; j := c; m := id[(d+c) div 2];
   while (i <= j) do
   begin
     while (names[id[i]] < names[m]) do inc(i);
     while (names[m] < names[id[j]]) do dec(j);
     if (i <= j) then
     begin
         t := id[i];
         id[i] := id[j];
         id[j] := t;
         inc(i); dec(j);
     end; // if i <= j
   end; // while i <= j
   if (d < j) then IdQuickSort(d,j);
   if (i < c) then IdQuickSort(i,c);
end; // IdQuickSort

function CodeSum(var s: str): int;
  var sum, i: int;
begin
  sum := 0;
  for i := 1 to length(s) do
    sum := sum + ord(s[i])-ord('A')+1;
```

```
      exit(sum);
end; // CodeSum

procedure E22;
  var i, score: int;
begin
  ReadInput;
  for i := 1 to n do id[i] := i;
  IdQuickSort(1,n);
  score := 0;
  for i := 1 to n do
    score := score + i*CodeSum(names[id[i]]);
  writeln(NL, ' Total Score: ', score);
end; // E22

BEGIN
  E22; // 871198282
  // ----------------------------
  writeln(NL, ' T H E    E N D .');
  readln;
end.
```

Java Program

```
/****************************************
    Problem 22: Score of names
    Answer = 871198282, Time = 0.02 sec.
****************************************/

import java.io.*;
import java.util.ArrayList;
import java.util.Collections;
import java.util.Iterator;

public class E22 {
 E22() throws IOException {
 readAndCompute();
 }

    private void readAndCompute() throws IOException {
    int MN = 6000;
    char [] a = new char[12*MN];
    ArrayList<String> names = new ArrayList<String>();
```

```java
    // Create a FileReader Object
     FileReader f = new FileReader("p022_names.txt");
f.read(a);    // reads the content to the array a
f.close();
String s = "";

// Split
for (char c : a) {
   if (c >= 'A' && c <= 'Z') {
     s += c;
   }
   else {
      if (s != "") { names.add(s); }
      s = "";
   }
} // for
Collections.sort(names);
int i = 0;
int score = 0;
for (String e : names) {
   ++i;
   int v = 0;
   a = e.toCharArray();
   for (char c : a) {
    v += (int)(c-'A'+1);
   } // for c
   score += i*v;
} // for e
   System.out.println("\n ** Result: " + score);
   //  871198282
} // for c
} // E22
```

Problem 23. Non-abundant sums

A *perfect number* is a number for which the sum of its proper divisors is exactly equal to the number. For example, the sum of the proper divisors of 28 would be $1 + 2 + 4 + 7 + 14 = 28$, which means that 28 is a perfect number.

A number n is called *deficient* if the sum of its proper divisors is less than n, and it is called *abundant* if this sum exceeds n.

As 12 is the smallest abundant number, $1 + 2 + 3 + 4 + 6 = 16$, the smallest number that can be written as the sum of two abundant numbers is 24. By mathematical analysis, it can be shown that all integers greater than 28123 can be written as the sum of two abundant numbers. However, this upper limit cannot be reduced any further by analysis even though it is known that the greatest number that cannot be expressed as the sum of two abundant numbers is less than this limit.

Find the sum of all the positive integers which cannot be written as the sum of two abundant numbers.

Understanding

Let $d(n)$ be the sum of proper divisors of n (numbers less than n which divide evenly into n, see Problem 21). Then we can classify all positive integers as follows:

For each positive integer n

- n is *perfect* if and only if $d(n) = n$.
- n is *deficient* if and only if $d(n) < n$.
- n is *abundant* if and only if $d(n) > n$.

We temporary call a positive integer an *AA number* (Abundant + Abundant) if it can be written as the sum of two abundant numbers.

The web site abundant number article on Wolfram informs that all integers greater than 20161 are AA. But the result of the Problem stays the same because $20161 < 28123$.

The Problem asks to find the following sum:

$$\text{sum } \{n \mid 1 \le n \le 28123, n \text{ is not AA}\}$$

Algorithm

Step 1. Compute $d(n)$ = sum of all proper divisors of n, for all n, $1 \le n \le \text{LIM} = 28123$ (see Problem 21). We construct a similar algorithm to Sieve of Eratosthenes as follows. For each natural number i from 1 to LIM div 2, we consider i as a divisor of all numbers $k \times i$ between $2 \times i$ and LIM, so we add i to the $d[k \times i]$.

```
Algorithm Setd
Input: integer LIM = 28123.
Output: d[1...LIM].
    d[i] = sum {a | a < i, i = k × a, 1 ≤ i ≤ LIM }
begin
    d[1] ← 0;
    // 1 is a proper divisor of all i > 1
    for i ← 2 to LIM do d[i] ← 1;
    for i ← 2 to LIM div 2 do
        for j ← (i + i) to LIM step i do
            d[j] ← d[j] + i;
        endfor j
    endfor i
    return d[ ];
endSetd
```

Note that if a is prime then $d(a) = 1$, so all primes are not abundant. They are deficient.

Step 2. Save all abundant numbers into array abund[] and mark them as abundant numbers.

```
Algorithm AllAbund
Input: integer LIM = 28123.
Output:  abund[1...count].
         d[abund[i]] > abund[i]
```

```
            1 ≤ i ≤ count
begin
    isAbund[] ← all false;
    count ← 0;
    for n ← 12 to LIM do
        if (d[n] > n) then
            // n is abundant
            count ← count + 1;
            abund[count] ← n;
            isAbund[n] ← true;
        endif
    endfor n
    return (abund[], count, isAbund[]);
endAllAbund
```

Step 3. Get sum$\{n \mid 1 \leq n \leq 28123, n$ is not AA$\}$

To test if a number n is AA, we take each abundant number a and check the condition:

$$\text{if } n - a \text{ is abundant then } n \text{ is AA}$$

```
Algorithm AA
Input:   integer n, 1 ≤ n ≤ LIM = 28123.
Output: if n is AA then true else false.
begin
    for each abundant number a in abund[]   do
        if (n−a) is abundant then return true endif;
    endfor
    return false;
endAA
```

Comment

To verify the number LIM1 = 20161 we need only show that all number n from 20162 to 28123 is AA. In the next programs we include function Test20161 for this checking.

C++ Program

```
/****************************************
  Problem 23. Non-abundant sums
  Answer = 4179871, Time = 0.17 sec.
****************************************/
#include <iostream>
#include <windows.h>
#include <bitset>

using namespace std;

const int LIM = 28123; // 20161

bitset<LIM+1> isAbund;
int abund[LIM+1]; // list of abundant numbers
int d[LIM+1]; // d[j] = sum of all proper divisors of j
int numberOfAbund; // total number of abundants

// d[j] = sum of all proper divisors of j
// d[j] = sum {i| i < j, i divides j}
// 1 <= j < LIM. See Problem 21
void Setd() {
   int i, j, n2 = LIM/2;
   d[1] = 0;
   for(i = 2; i <= LIM; ++i) d[i] = 1;//Init all 1
   for(i = 2; i <= n2; ++i) {
      for (j = i + i; j <= LIM; j += i) {
         // j = k*i -> i divides j
         d[j] += i;
         // d[j] = sum {i| i < j, i | j}
      } // for j
   } // for i
} // setd

// Get all abundant numbers into abund[]
void AllAbund() {
   int n;
   numberOfAbund = 0;
   isAbund.reset();
   for (n = 12; n <= LIM; ++n) {
      if (d[n] > n) {
         abund[++numberOfAbund] = n;
         isAbund[n] = 1;
```

```
    } // if
  } // for
} // AllAbund

// n = abund + abund
bool AA(int n) {
   int n2 = n/2;
   for (int i = 1; i <= numberOfAbund; ++i) {
      if (abund[i] > n2) return false;
      // abund[i] <= n2
      if (isAbund[n-abund[i]] == 1) return true;
   } // for
   return false;
} // AA

void E23() {
   int n;
   Setd();
   AllAbund();
   int sum = 0;
   for (n = 1; n <= LIM; ++n)
    if (!AA(n)) sum += n;
   cout << "\n Answer = " << sum;
} // E23

void Test20161() {
   int n;
   int c = 0; // counting not AA
   const int LIM1 = 20161;
   for (n = LIM1+1; n <= LIM; ++n)
      // n is AA = abund + abund ?
      if (!AA(n)) ++c;
   cout << "\n Test for 20161 c = " << c;
   if (c > 0) cout << "\n Incorrect.";
    else cout << "\n Correct.";
} // Test20161

main() {
  E23();   // 4179871
  Test20161();
  cout << "\n  T H E    E N D .";
  return 0;
}
```

Free Pascal Program

```
(*************************************
   Problem 23. Non-abundant sums
   Answer = 4179871, Time = 0.17 sec.
*************************************)

const NL = #13#10;
LIM = 28123; // 20161
type int = longint;
var
   IsAbund: array[1..LIM] of boolean;
   d, abund: array[0..LIM+1] of int;
   // abund: List of abundant numbers
   numberOfAbund: int;

// The sum of all proper divisors of n
procedure Setd;
  var i, j, n2: int;
begin
   d[1] := 0; n2 := LIM div 2;
   for i := 1 to LIM do d[i] := 1;//Init all 1
   for i := 2 to n2 do
   begin
    j := i + i;
      while (j <= LIM) do
      begin
        d[j] := d[j] + i;
        // d[j] = sum {i| i < j, i divides j}
        j := j + i;
      end; // while
   end; // for
end; // setd

// Get all abundant numbers into abund[]
procedure AllAbund;
  var n: int;
begin
   numberOfAbund := 0;
   fillchar(isAbund, sizeof(isAbund), false);
   for n := 12 to LIM do
     if (d[n] > n) then
     begin
        inc(numberOfAbund);
```

```
         abund[numberOfAbund] := n;
         isAbund[n] := true;
   end; // if
end; // AllAbund

// n = abund + abund
function AA(n: int): boolean;
 var n2, i: int;
begin
   n2 := n div 2;
   for i := 1 to numberOfAbund do
   begin
      if (abund[i] > n2) then exit(false);
      // abund[i] <= n2
      if (isAbund[n-abund[i]]) then exit(true);
   end; // for
   exit(false);
end; // AA

procedure E23;
 var n, sum: int;
begin
   Setd;
   AllAbund;
   sum := 0;
   for n := 1 to LIM do
     if Not(AA(n)) then sum := sum + n;
   writeln(NL, ' Answer = ', sum);
end; // E23

procedure Test20161;
 var n: int;
 c: int;
 const LIM1 = 20161;
begin
 c := 0; // counting not AA
 for n := LIM1+1 to LIM do
   // n is AA = abund + abund ?
   if Not(AA(n)) then inc(c);
 writeln(NL, ' Test for 20161 c = ', c);
 if (c > 0) then writeln(' Incorrect.')
   else writeln(NL, ' Correct.');
end; // Test20161
```

```
BEGIN
  E23;   // 4179871
  Test20161; // Correct
  writeln(NL, '  T H E    E N D . ');
  readln;
END.
```

Java Program

```
/**************************************
   Problem 23. Non-abundant sums
   Answer = 4179871, Time = 0.17 sec.
**************************************/
import java.util.BitSet;
public class E23 {
private int LIM = 28123; // can use 20161
private BitSet isAbund = new BitSet(LIM+1);
private int [] abund  = new int[LIM+1];
private int [] d = new int[LIM+1];
private int numberOfAbund;

E23() {
   setd();
   allAbund();
   System.out.println(getSum()); // 4179871
   test20161();
}

// d[j] = sum of all proper divisors of j
// d[j] = sum {i| i < j, i divides j}
// 1 <= j < LIM. See Problem 21
private void setd() {
   int n2 = LIM/2;
   d[1] = 0;
   for(int i = 2; i <= LIM; ++i)
    d[i] = 1;//Init all 1
   for(int i = 2; i <= n2; ++i) {
     for (int j = i + i; j <= LIM; j += i) {
        // j = k*i -> i divides j
        d[j] += i;
        // d[j] = sum {i| i < j, i divides j}
     } // for j
   } // for i
```

```
}  // setd

// Get all abundant numbers into abund[]
void allAbund() {
   int n = 0;
   numberOfAbund = 0;
   for (n = 12; n <= LIM; ++n) {
      if (d[n] > n) {
         abund[++numberOfAbund] = n;
         isAbund.set(n);
      }  // if
   }  // for
}  // allAbund

private int getSum() {
   int sum = 0;
   for (int n = 1; n <= LIM; ++n)
    if (!AA(n)) sum += n;
   return sum;
}  // getSum

// n = abund + abund
private boolean AA(int n) {
  int n2 = n/2;
   for (int i = 1; i <= numberOfAbund; ++i) {
      if (abund[i] > n2) return false;
      // abund[i] <= n2
      if (isAbund.get(n-abund[i])) return true;
   }  // for
   return false;
}  // AA

private void test20161() {
   int n;
   int c = 0;  // counting not AA
   int LIM1 = 20161;
   for (n = LIM1+1; n <= LIM; ++n)
    // n is AA = abund + abund ?
    if (!AA(n)) ++c;
   System.out.println("\n Test for 20161 c = " + c);
   if (c > 0) System.out.println("\n Incorrect.");
    else System.out.println("\n Correct.");
}  // test20161
}  // class E23
```

Problem 24. Lexicographic permutations

A permutation is an ordered arrangement of objects. For example, 3124 is one possible permutation of the digits 1, 2, 3 and 4. If all of the permutations are listed numerically or alphabetically, we call it *lexicographic order.* The lexicographic permutations of 0, 1 and 2 are:

  012 021 102 120 201 210

What is the 1000000th lexicographic permutation of the digits 0, 1, 2, 3, 4, 5, 6, 7, 8 and 9?

Understanding

Let $S = \{0, 1, ..., n-1\}$ be an ordered set of n digits 0, 1, ..., $n-1$, $1 \le n \le 10$. We know that there are $n!$ permutations in total, and these permutations can be listed alphabetically in a list, which denoted by $L(S)$. Tab. 24.1 shows the list $L(S)$, where $S = \{0, 1, 2, 3\}$, $n = 4$. The function $n! = 1 \times 2 \times ... \times n$ is called the *factorial* of n, $n \ge 0$, (accepted $0! = 1$.)

There are two popular problems concerning the permutations:

Problem No 1 (PosToPer). Given an ordered set S and a position t of a lexicographic permutation p in $L(S)$, $t = \text{Pos}(p, L(S))$. Find permutation p? For example, given $S = \{0, 1, 2, 3\}$ and $t = 20$. Find permutation p such that $\text{Pos}(p, L(S)) = 20$. Answer: PosToPer(20) = 3102.

Problem No 2 (PerToPos). Given an ordered set S and a lexicographic permutation p of S. Find *position* of p, $\text{Pos}(p, L(S))$, in the lexicographic list $L(S)$? For example, given $S = \{0, 1, 2, 3\}$ and $p = 3102$. Find $\text{Pos}(p, L(S))$. Answer: PerToPos(3102) = 20.

N	Perm.	N	Perm.	N	Perm.	N	Perm.
0	0123	6	1023	12	2013	18	3012
1	0132	7	1032	13	2031	19	3021
2	0213	8	1203	14	2103	20	**3102**
3	0231	9	1230	15	2130	21	3120
4	0312	10	1302	16	2301	22	3201
5	0321	11	1320	17	2310	23	3210

Tab. 24.1 *Lexicographic list of all permutations of n = 4.*

In general, problem 24 states that: Given $S = \{0, 1, 2, 3, 4, 5, 6, 7, 8, 9\}$. Find m^{th} lexicographic permutation p? Because the order of elements in list $L(S)$ is started at 1, the answer will be PosToPer($m-1$).

	PosToPer	PerToPos
Given	n, S, t	n, S, p
Find	p	t

Problems of permutations

Algorithm

Suppose that $S = \{0, 1, \ldots, n-1\}$. There are $n!$ permutations numbered from 0 to $n! - 1$.

We give two solving versions for this Problem. Recall that our goal is constructing the algorithm PosToPer. The first version, E24A is based on the sequential generation of permutations from the first (unit) permutation $p_{min} = (0, 1, \ldots, n-1)$ to the last (maximum) permutation $p_{max} = (n-1, \ldots, 1, 0)$. (Edsger W. Dijkstra, W.H. Feijen, "*A Method of Programming*", Published January 1st 1988 by Addison Wesley Longman.)

The second version, E24B is based on the method of directly computing the permutation for each giving its position in the lexicographic list.

Version E24A

Let $S = \{0, 1, \ldots, n-1\}$, $n \geq 1$. Starting with the first permutation, called the *unit permutation*, $p = (0, 1, \ldots, n-1)$, we repeat calling function Next for 999999 times to get the 1000000th permutation.

Algorithm E24A

Input: integer n ≤ 10, integer t: 1 ≤ t ≤ n!.
Output: Lexicographic permutation
        at position t: p = (x₀, x₁, xₙ₋₁).
begin
    // Initialize the unit permutation
    set p ← (0, 1, ..., n−1);
    repeat t−1 times
        Next; // p ← Next p
    endrepeat
    return p;
endE24A

Let $p = (x_0, x_1, \ldots, x_{n-1})$ be a permutation of n numbers in S. To find the next permutation $p' > p$ in the lexicographic list of all permutations of n, $L(S)$, we process as follows:

Step 1   Scan from $n-1$ backward to 0 to find the latest index i such that $x_i < x_{i+1}$.
         If such i does not exist, then p is the maximum permutation,
         $p = (n-1, n-2, \ldots, 0)$, and, of course, p' does not exist: return false.
Step 2   (*There is an i such that $x_i < x_{i+1}$.*)
         Scan again from $n-1$ backward to $i+1$ to find the latest index j
         such that $x_i < x_j$.
Step 3   Swap x_i and x_j.
Step 4   Reverse the last segment (postfix) $p(i+1 \ldots n-1)$.
Step 5   Return p as the next permutation (p').

Algorithm Next

Input: integer n,
       Lexicographic permutation p[0...n−1] in position t.
Output: Lexicographic permutation p'[0...n−1] in position t+1.
        true if there is exist p'; else false.

```
begin
    for i ← n−2 down to 0 do
        if (p[i] < p[i+1]) then break for;
    endfor;
    if (i < 0) return (p, false);
    // p[i] < p[i+1]
    for j ← n−1 down to i+1 do
        if (p[j] > p[i]) then break for;
    endfor;
    // p[j] > p[i]
    Swap(p[i], p[j]);
    Reverse segment p[i+1, n−1].
    return (p, true);
endNext
```

Tab. 24.2 demonstrates the algorithm for finding the next permutation p' of the given permutation $p = (7, 8, 3, 6, 5, 1, 4, 2, 0)$, $n = 9$.

position	0	1	2	3	4	5	6	7	8
p	7	8	3	6	5	1	4	2	0
Step 1: i = 5	7	8	3	6	5	**1**	4	2	0
Step 2: j = 7	7	8	3	6	5	1	4	**2**	0
Step 3:	7	8	3	6	5	**2**	4	**1**	0
Step 4:	7	8	3	6	5	2	<u>0</u>	<u>1</u>	<u>4</u>

Tab. 24.2 *Finding the next permutation p' of p.*

p = (7,8,3,6,5,1,4,2,0), p' = (7,8,3,6,5,2,0,1,4).

With $n = 10$, algorithm Next needs 2 times scanning 10 elements, and algorithm E24A needs one million of calling Next. Therefore, version E24A needs 20 million comparative and assignment times.

C++ Program

```
/ * * * * * * * * * * * * * * * * * * * * * * * * * * * * * * * * * * * * * * * * * *
    Problem 24. Lexicographic permutations
    Version E24A.
    Answer = 2783915460, Time = 0.27 sec.
* * * * * * * * * * * * * * * * * * * * * * * * * * * * * * * * * * * * * * * * * * /
```

```cpp
#include <iostream>

using namespace std;

const int MN = 12;
int p[MN];
int n; // n = 10 elements 0...9

// Print permutation p
void Print(const char * msg = "") {
   cout << msg;
   for (int i = 0; i < n; ++i)
    cout << p[i];
}// Print

void Swap(int i, int j) {
   int t = p[i];
   p[i] = p[j];
   p[j] = t;
} // Swap

// Next permutation
bool Next() {
   int i, j;
   // Step 1. Find the last i: p[i] < p[i+1]
   for (i = n-2; i >= 0 ;--i)
    if (p[i] < p[i+1]) break;

   if (i < 0) return false; // p is the max permutation

   // Step 2. Find the last j: p[j] > p[i]
   for (j = n-1; p[j] <= p[i]; --j) ;

   Swap(i,j); // Step 3.

   // Step 4. Reverse p[i+1...n-1]
   ++i; j = n-1;
   while(i < j) { Swap(i,j); ++i; --j; }
   return true; // Step 5.
}// Next

void E24A() {
   int i;
   n = 10;
```

```
  // Init: p[i] = i
  for (i = 0; i < n; ++i) p[i] = i;
  // Repeat 999999 times
  for (i = 1; i < 1000000; ++i) Next();
  Print("\n Result E24A: ");
} // E24A

main() {
  E24A(); // 2783915460
  //---------------------------
  cout << "\n T H E    E N D.";
  return 0;
}
```

Free Pascal Program

```
(***********************************************
   Problem 24. Lexicographic permutations
   Version E24A.
   Answer = 2783915460, Time = 0.27 sec.
***********************************************)

const NL = #13#10; BL = #32; MN = 12;

type int = longint;
TA = array[0..MN] of int;
var
  p: TA; // permutation p[0..n-1]
  n: int;

// Print permutation p[0..n-1]
procedure Print(msg: string);
  var i: int;
begin
  write(msg);
    for i := 0 to n-1 do write(p[i]);
  end; // Print

  procedure Swap(i, j: int);
    var t: int;
  begin
    t := p[i]; p[i] := p[j]; p[j] := t;
  end; // Swap
```

```
// Next permutation
function Next: Boolean;
  var i, j, k: int;
begin
// Step 1. Find the last index i: p[i] < p[i+1].
i := -1;
for  k := n-2 downto 0 do
  if (p[k] < p[k+1]) then
  begin
  i := k;
  break;
  end;
// p[i] < p[i+1]
if (i < 0) then exit(false);
// Step 2. Find the last index j: p[j] > p[i].
for k := n-1 downto i+1 do
  if p[k] > p[i] then
  begin
  j := k;
  break;
  end;
Swap(i,j); // Step 3.
// Step 4. Reverse p[i+1..n-1]
inc(i); j := n-1;
while(i < j) do
begin
   Swap(i,j);
   inc(i); dec(j);
end;
exit(true); // Step 5.
end; // Next

procedure  E24A;
  var i: int;
begin
n := 10;
// Init: set unit permutation
for i := 0 to n-1 do p[i] := i;
// Repeat 999999 times
for i := 1 to 999999 do Next;
Print(NL+' Result E24A: ');
end; // E24A
BEGIN
  E24A;
```

```
   //----------------------------
   writeln(NL, ' T H E     E N D .');
   readln;
END.
```

Java Program

```
/***********************************************
   Problem 24. Lexicographic permutations
   Version E24A.
   Answer = 2783915460, Time = 0.27 sec.
***********************************************/
public class E24 {
   private int MN = 10;
   private int [] p = new int[MN];
   private int n = 10; // 10 element: 0...n-1

   E24() {
    e24A(); // 2783915460
    }

   public void e24A() {
    int i;
    n = 10;
    // Init: Init unit permutation
    for (i = 0; i < n; ++i) p[i] = i;
    // Repeat 999999 times
    for (i = 1; i < 1000000; ++i) next();
    System.out.print("\n Result of E24A : ");
    for (int e: p) System.out.print(e);//2783915460
    } // e24A

   // Next permutation
   private boolean next() {
       int i, j, t;
       // Step1. Find the last index i: p[i] < p[i+1]
       for (i = n-2; i >= 0 ;--i)
         if (p[i] < p[i+1]) break;
       if (i < 0) return false;
       // Step 2.Find the last index j: p[j] > p[i].
       for (j = n-1; p[j] <= p[i]; --j) ;
       // Step 3. Swap p[i] and p[j]
       t = p[i]; p[i] = p[j]; p[j] = t;
       // Step 4. Reverse p[i+1..n-1]
```

```
    ++i; j = n-1;
    while(i < j) {
      t = p[i]; p[i] = p[j]; p[j] = t;
      ++i; --j;
    }
    return true; // Step 5.
  } // Next
} // class E24
```

Version E24B

Let n be a positive integer, and $S = \{0, 1, \ldots, n-1\}$ be an ordered set of digits $0, 1, \ldots, n-1$. Let $L(S)$ be the lexicographic ordered list of all $n!$ permutations of S. Suppose that t is a position (started at 0) in $L(S)$. If we know t then we can compute t^{th} permutation $p = (x_0, x_1, \ldots, x_{n-1})$ in n steps, step i gives x_i, $0 \le i \le n-1$, and needs only two divisions.

Let $p = (x_0, x_1, \ldots, x_{n-1})$ be a permutation in $L(S)$. We divide $L(S)$ into n *groups* (or *classes*) by the first element x_0 and consider the following relation:

Two permutations $u = (u_0, u_1, \ldots, u_{n-1})$ and $v = (v_0, v_1, \ldots, v_{n-1})$

are in the same group $[i]$ if and only if $u_0 = v_0 = i$.

Therefore, each permutation in the group $[i]$ has the form $(i, *, \ldots, *)$, where all $*$ are different elements in the set $S-\{i\}$. Now we have n groups, each group has $(n-1)!$ permutations.

Example

Let $n = 4$, $S = \{0, 1, 2, 3\}$. All $4! = 24$ permutations of $L(S)$ is listed geographically in Tab. 24.3.

Let $p = (x_0, x_1, \ldots, x_{n-1})$ be a permutation in $L(S)$. Denote by

$$\text{Tail}([x_0]) = \{(x_1, \ldots, x_{n-1}) \mid (x_0, x_1, \ldots, x_{n-1}) \in [x_0]\}.$$

We see that $\text{Tail}([x_0])$ is the list of all $(n-1)!$ permutations of $S-\{x_0\}$.

At this point we know that:

- If $S = \{0, 1, \ldots, n-1\}$, $n \ge 1$, $0 \le t < n!$ and $p = (x_0, x_1, \ldots, x_{n-1})$ is the permutation at the position t in $L(S)$ then $p \in [x_0]$,

- The position of x_0 in S is $Pos(x_0, S) = t$ div $(n-1)!$. So x_0 is the element at position t div $(n-1)!$ in S.
- The position of p in the group $[x_0]$ is $Pos(p, S-\{x_0\}) = t$ mod $(n-1)!$.

N	Perm.	N	Perm.	N	Perm.	N	Perm.
Group [0]		Group [1]		Group [2]		Group [3]	
0	0123	6	1023	12	2013	18	3012
1	0132	7	1032	13	2031	19	3021
2	0213	8	1203	14	2103	20	3102
3	0231	9	1230	15	2130	21	3120
4	0312	10	1302	16	2301	22	3201
5	0321	11	1320	17	2310	23	3210

Tab. 24.3 *Four groups of permutations of n = 4.*

After getting x_0, in the next step we will find x_1 with $n = n-1$, $t = t$ mod $(n-1)!$ and $S = S-\{x_0\}, \ldots$

The next algorithm, PosToPer, gives lexicographic permutation of n, $p = (x_0, x_1, \ldots, x_{n-1})$ knowing its position t.

```
Algorithm PosToPer
Input: integer n ≤ 10, 0 ≤ t < n!.
Output:  Lexicographic permutation
         at position t, p = (x₀, x₁, …, xₙ₋₁).
begin
    m ← n; S ← {0, …, n−1};
    for i ← 0 to n−1 do
    // compute xᵢ
        m ← m − 1;
        e ← t div (m!);
        xᵢ ← GetElem(e) in S;
        S ← S − {xᵢ};
        t ← t mod (m!);
    endfor
    return p;
endPosToPer
```

Note that the Problem gives ordered number t started at 1, so the answer of the problem will be PosToPer($t-1$).

The next example demonstrates how to get elements x_0, x_1, ..., x_{n-1} of p.

Example

Given $n = 4$, $S = \{0, 1, 2, 3\}$. Let all the permutations of n numbers in S be sorted in the lexicographic order $L(S)$ (Tab. 24.3). We want to find 21st permutation $p = (x_0, x_1, x_2, x_3)$ in $L(S)$. Note that in Tab. 24.3 the 21st permutation has position 20, so we begin with $t = 20$ (Tab. 24.4).

i	m	t	m!	e = t div m!	x	S
	4	20				{0:0, 1:1, 2:2, 3:3}
0	3	20	6	3	3	{0:0, 1:1, 2:2}
1	2	2	2	1	1	{0:0, 1:2}
2	1	0	1	0	0	{0:2}
3	0	0	1	0	2	{}

Tab. 24.4 Computing 21th permutation
p = 3102, t = 20.

To get final programs we need only construct two simple supporting algorithms Factorial and GetElem.

First at all, we give factorials for the first ten numbers, fac(i), $0 \le i \le 9$ (Tab. 24.5). Note that, for convenience we accept that $0! = 1$.

n	0	1	2	3	4	5	6	7	8	9
n!	1	1	2	6	24	120	720	5040	40320	362880

Tab. 24.5 Factorials of n, $0 \le n < 10$

```
Algorithm AllFac
Input: integer n ≤ 9.
Output: fac[0] = 1, fac[i] = i × fac[i−1], 1 ≤ i ≤ n.
begin
    fac[0] ← 1;
    for i ← 1 to n do
        fac[i] ← i × fac[i−1];
    endfor
    return fac[];
endAllFac
```

The ordered set $S = \{0, 1, \ldots, n-1\}$ can be represent as a bit sequence S, where $S[i] = 1$ means that i is an element in S and otherwise, $S[i] = 0$ means that the number i does not belong S.

	0	1	2	3	4	5	6	7	8	9
S	1	0	0	1	1	0	0	0	0	1

Tab. 24.6 *The ordered set S = {0:0, 1:3, 2:4, 3:9}.*

To insert element e to S, we set $S[e] = 1$, and to delete element e from S, we set $S[e] = 0$. To get the element at position t in S we simply count t numbers 1 in S beginning from index 0 and then return the index i, where $S[i] = 1$ and counter $= t$.

```
Algorithm GetElem
Input: Ordered set S, integers n, t.
Output: Element e at position t in
            ordered set S.
begin
    count ← −1;
    for i ← 0 to n do
        count ← count + S[i];
        if (count = t) then return i endif;
    endfor
endGetElem
```

Algorithm PerToPos is a symmetry of algorithm PosToPer.

Algorithm PerToPos

Input: integer n > 0,
           Ordered set S = {0, 1, ..., n−1},
              p = (x₀, x₁, ..., xₙ₋₁) in L(S).
Output: 0 ≤ t < n! .
              t: position of p in L(S).
begin
   m ← n−1;
   set all 0 to array used[ ];
   t ← GetPos(p[m]);
   for i = n−2 downto 0 do
      t ← GetPos(p[i]) × (m−i)! + t;
   endfor
   return t;
endPerToPos

Algorithm GetPos is a symmetry of algorithm GetElem.

Algorithm GetPos

Input: Element e in ordered set S,
            integer n = #S.
Output: integer t.
begin
   count ← 0; used[e] ← 1;
   for i ← 0 to e−1 do
      count ← count + used[i];
   endfor
   return count;
endGetPos

C++ Program

```
/ * * * * * * * * * * * * * * * * * * * * * * * * * * * * * * * * * * * * * * * * * * * * *
   Problem 24. Lexicographic permutations
   Version E24B.
```

255 | LEARNING THROUGH PROJECT EULER

```
   Answer = 2783915460, Time = 0.1 sec.
*********************************************/
#include <iostream>
#include <windows.h>
using namespace std;

const int MN = 12;
int p[MN];
int n; // n = 10 elements: 0...(n-1)
bool used[MN]; // used[e] = true if number e is takeout
int fac[MN]; // fac[i] = i!, 0 <= i < 10

// Print permutation p[0..n-1]
void Print(const char * msg = "") {
   cout << msg;
   for (int i = 0; i < n; ++i)
     cout << p[i];
} // Print

// Get unused sth number
int GetPos(int e) {
  int i, s;
   s = 0; used[e] = 1;
   for (i = 0; i < e; ++i) {
     s += used[i];
   }
   return s;
}  // GetPos

int GetElem(int v) {
   int i, d = -1;
   for (i = 0; i < n; ++i) {
     d += used[i]; // used[i] is in {0, 1}
     if (d == v) {
      used[i] = 0;
      return i;
     } // if
   } // for
} // GetElem

// Get permutation t-th
void PosToPer(int t) {
   int i, m = n;
   for (i = 0; i < n; ++i) used[i] = 1;
```

```
    for (i = 0; i < n; ++i) {
      --m;
      p[i] = GetElem(t/fac[m]);
      t %= fac[m];
    } // for
} // PosToPer

// Get position of permutation p
// in the lexicographic list of
// all permutations of n numbers 0...(n-1)
int PerToPos(const char * per) {
  int t, i, m = n-1;
  n = strlen(per);
  // Init
  for (i = 0; i < n; ++i) {
    p[i] = per[i]-'0';
    used[i] = 0;
  }
  t = GetPos(p[m]);
  for (i = n-2; i >= 0; --i) {
    t = GetPos(p[i])*fac[m-i] + t;
  } // for
  return t;
} // PerToPos
// All factorial(i) = i!, 0 <= i < n
void Init(int nn) {
  int i;
  n = nn;
  fac[0] = fac[1] = 1;
  for (i = 2; i < n; ++i)
    fac[i] = fac[i-1]*i;
} // Init
void E24B() {
  Init(10);
  PosToPer(999999); // 2783915460
  Print("\n Result E24B: ");
} // E24B
main() {
  E24B(); // 2783915460
  cout << "\n " << PerToPos("2783915460")+1;
  //--------------------------
  cout << "\n T H E    E N D.";
  return 0;
}
```

Free Pascal Program

```
(**********************************************
   Problem 24. Lexicographic permutations
   Version E24B
   Answer = 2783915460 , Time = 0.1 sec.
**********************************************)

const NL = #13#10; BL = #32; MN = 12;

type int = longint;

TA = array[0..MN] of int;
var
   p: TA; // permutation
   fac: TA; // factorial
   n: int;
   used: array[0..MN] of byte;

// Print permutation p[0..n-1]
procedure Print(msg: string);
   var i: int;
begin
   write(msg);
   for i := 0 to n-1 do write(p[i]);
end; // Print

// Get position of permutation p
// in lexicographic list of all permutations of n
function GetPos(e: int): int;
   var i, s: int;
begin
   s := 0; used[e] := 1;
   for i := 0 to e-1 do s := s + used[i];
   exit(s);
end; // GetPos

// Get unused number v-th
function GetElem(v: int): int;
   var i, d: int;
begin
   d := -1;
   for i := 0 to n-1 do
   begin
```

```
      d := d + used[i];
      if (d = v) then
      begin
       used[i] := 0;
       exit(i);
      end; // if
   end; // for
end; // GetElem

// Get permutation t-th
// in the lexicographic list
// of all permutations of n
procedure  PosToPer(t: int);
   var i, m: int;
begin
   for i := 0 to n-1 do used[i] := 1;
   m := n;
   for i := 0 to n-1 do
   begin
     dec(m);
     p[i] := GetElem(t div fac[m]);
     t := t mod fac[m];
   end; // for
end; // PosToPer

// Get position of permutation p
function PerToPos(hv: string): int;
   var i, t, m: int;
begin
   n := length(hv);
   // Init
   for i := 1 to n do
   begin
     p[i-1] := ord(hv[i])-ord('0');
     used[i-1] := 0;
   end;
   m := n-1;
   t := GetPos(p[m]);
   for i := n-2 downto 0 do
     t := GetPos(p[i])*fac[m-i] + t;
   exit(t);
end; // PerToPos

// Init n
```

```
// fac[i] = i!, 0 <= i < n.
procedure  Init(nn: int);
   var i: int;
begin
   n := nn;
   fac[0] := 1; fac[1] := 1;
   for i := 2 to n-1 do  fac[i] := fac[i-1]*i;
end; // Init

procedure  E24B;
begin
   Init(10);
   PosToPer(999999); // 2783915460
   Print(NL+' Result E24B: ');
end; // E24B

BEGIN
   E24B;
   writeln(NL, BL, BL , PerToPos('2783915460')+1);
   //---------------------------
   writeln(NL, ' T H E   E N D .');
   readln;
END.
```

Java Program

```
/***********************************************
   Problem 24. Lexicographic permutations
   Version e24B.
   Answer = 2783915460, Time = 0.1 sec.
***********************************************/
import java.util.BitSet;
public class E24 {
   private int MN = 10;
   private int p[] = new int[MN];
   private int n = 10; // n = 10 elements: 0...9
   BitSet used = new BitSet(MN+2);
   private int [] fac = new int[MN+2];

E24() {
   e24B(); // 2783915460
   System.out.print("\n ** " +
            (perToPos("2783915460")+1));
}
```

```
private void e24B() {
   setFac(10);
   posToPer(999999);
   System.out.print("\n * Result of E24B : ");
   for (int e: p)
      System.out.print(e); // 2783915460
} // e24B

// Factorial(i), 1 <= i <= n-1
private void setFac(int nn) {
   int i;
   n = nn;
   fac[0] = fac[1] = 1;
   for (i = 2; i < n; ++i) {
      fac[i] = fac[i-1]*i;
   }
} // SetFac

private void posToPer(int t) {
   for (int i = 0; i < n; ++i) {
      used.set(i);
   }
   int m = n-1;
   for (int i = 0; i < n; ++i) {
      p[i] = getElem(t/fac[m-i]);
      t %= fac[m-i];
   }
} // PosToPer

// Get position of permutation p
// in the lexicographic list of
// all permutations of n numbers 0...(n-1)
private int perToPos(String per) {
   int t = 0, m = n-1;
   int n = per.length();
   // Convert per to p
   for (int i = 0; i < n; ++i)
      p[i] = (int)per.charAt(i)-'0';
   t = getPos(p[m]);
   for (int i = n-2; i >= 0; --i) {
      t = getPos(p[i])*fac[m-i] + t;
   } // for
   return t;
```

```
    }   // PerToPos

// Get unused s-th number
private int getPos(int e) {
    int i, s = 0;
    s = 0; used.set(e);
    for (i = 0; i < e; ++i) {
        if (used.get(i)) ++s;
    }
    return s;
}   // getPos

private int getElem(int v) {
    int d = -1;
    for (int i = 0; i < n; ++i) {
        d += (used.get(i)) ? 1 : 0;
        if (d == v) {
            used.clear(i);
            return i;
        }
    }
    return 0;
}   // getElem
}   // class E24
```

Problem 25. 1000-digit Fibonacci number

The Fibonacci sequence is defined by the recurrence relation:

$F_n = F_{n-1} + F_{n-2}$, where $F_1 = 1$ and $F_2 = 1$.

Hence the first 12 terms will be:

$F_1 = 1, F_2 = 1, F_3 = 2, F_4 = 3, F_5 = 5, F_6 = 8,$

$F_7 = 13, F_8 = 21, F_9 = 34, F_{10} = 55, F_{11} = 89, F_{12} = 144$

The 12th term, F_{12}, is the first term to contain three digits.

What is the index of the first term in the Fibonacci sequence to contain 1000 digits?

Algorithm

Denote by #x the number of digits of a positive integer x. For example, #1024 = 4, #1000 = 4, #7 = 1, #0 = 1.

We know that:

$$\#x = \text{int}(\lg(x)) + 1$$

where logarithm, lg is on the base 10, int(x) gives the integer part of a real number x, for example, $\text{int}(3) = 3$, $\text{int}(3.9) = 3$, $\text{int}(0.022) = 0$.

In the Fibonacci sequence, the nth term, F_n satisfies the following condition:

$$\phi^{n-2} \le F_n \le \phi^{n-1}, where\ \phi = \frac{1 + \sqrt{5}}{2} \qquad (25.1)$$

(Knuth D., *The Art of Programming*, V. 1, Addison-Wesley, 1968)

(25.1) gives,

$$\lg \phi^{n-2} \le \lg F_n \le \lg \phi^{n-1}$$

$$(n - 2)\lg \phi \le \lg F_n \le (n - 1)\lg \phi$$

$$n - 2 \le \frac{\lg F_n}{\lg \phi} \le n - 1$$

In the other hand, we know that #F_n = 1000, so

$$\text{int}(\lg F_n) + 1 = 1000, \text{ or}$$

$$\text{int}(\lg F_n) = 999$$

Denote by $a = \frac{\lg F_n}{\lg \phi}$, we have $a = 4780.19$. Therefore, $4781.19 \le n \le 4782.19$. Since n is a positive integer, $n = 4782$.

C++ Program

```
/************************************************
   Problem 25. 1000-digit Fibonacci number
   Answer = 4782, Time = 0.09 sec.
************************************************/
#include <iostream>
#include <cmath>

using namespace std;

void E25() {
   float logphi = log10((1 + sqrt(5.0))/2); // 1.61803
   int n = (int)(999 / logphi) + 2;
   cout << endl << n;
}

main() {
   E25(); // 4782
   //---------------------------
   cout << "\n T H E    E N D.";
   return 0;
}
```

Free Pascal Program

```
(************************************************
   Problem 25. 1000-digit Fibonacci number
   Answer = 4782, Time = 0.09 sec.
************************************************)

uses math;

procedure E25;
var logphi: extended;
    n: integer;
begin
   logphi := log10((1 + sqrt(5))/2); // 1.61803
```

```
  n := trunc((999 / logphi)) + 2;
  writeln(n);
end;

BEGIN
  E25; // 4782
  //---------------------------
  writeln(#13#10, ' T H E    E N D. ');
  readln;
END.
```

Java Program

```
/************************************************
   Problem 25. 1000-digit Fibonacci number
   Answer = 4782, Time = 0.09 sec.
************************************************/
public class E25 {
   E25() {
      double logphi = log10((1.0
      + (double)Math.sqrt(5.0))/2.0);
      // logphi = 1.61803
      int n = (int)(999 / logphi) + 2;
      System.out.println(n); // a = 4780
   } // E25

   // In Java log is the natural logarithm.
   private double log10(double x) {
      return Math.log(x)/Math.log(10);
   } // log10
} // E25
```

26 - Mar - 2019

Printed in Great Britain
by Amazon